CLEAN ARCHITECTURE

Advanced Methods and Strategies to Software and Programming using Clean Architecture Theories

WILLIAM VANCE

Table of Contents

Introduction

In the last few months, I've been thinking a lot about software architecture, development patterns, solutions that end up being complex to maintain due to over-engineering and other everyday problems that I encounter in my work.

Several projects I worked on had patterns that were lost over time and others had generated an overload of technologies and patterns that made them more complex to maintain, even by more experienced people with time on their hands.

Because of this, I decided to start a series of books, covering a view of the responsibility of a clean software architect and how his performance can affect the quality of delivery, in addition to addressing the most used development standards and best practices.

Architecture

First of all, what is software architecture? No, it's not a set of techniques for Minecraft - although I really like the game.

Several authors have already given different definitions for software architecture, such as:

"The concept of the highest level of a system in its environment [...] the organization or structure of significant components interacting through interfaces so that these most important components are composed of successively smaller components and interfaces". "Part of the systems that are difficult to modify" - Martin Fowler

If we look for other authors or sources of information, we will have more concepts, but they all end up converging to a common point, which I summarize as:

Someone who defines and monitors the evolution of the software, both technically and at the process level. An architect who cares only about the technical part of the project - is not connected to it as a whole, and will fail.

The software development process has as a main analogy a factory mat, where the parts have been passing. Each one does his part and, in the end, something is delivered to the customer, always following the same process. Something wrong? Certainly. The mat is always producing, but in the same way as yesterday, always repeating. Software is something that changes, evolves in a few hours.

The variables change, and quickly. The formula developed this morning may no longer be valid at the end of the day, inclusive.

And I am not only referring to technology but processes and experience. The user is getting more demanding every day.

Software that we delivered years ago that only changed in cases of bugs, all procedural and full of forms, no longer sells - it is extinct! Just like that architect which only sets standards, places them on an intranet and only answers a few emails as well.

Something that has already been consolidated in projects outside the country (mainly in startups) and is now increasingly stronger here in the USA is that the responsibility for the entire architecture lies with a team as a whole. The architect is a highly experienced professional.

It would be a step above a senior software engineer, but he is not the only one responsible for the technology of the project - he is also, in some cases, responsible for being "accountable" for the project. A common question for those who see this model is, "Where are the managers?"

The real question is, "But what are they really for?" A mature team not only knows how to manage its time and tasks without a manager but also to monitor and discuss the evolution of its products, whether in technical or business terms.

The architect is just like a leader who helps to organize and guide the team, but it must be able to walk independently, not distorting its objectives and processes, but instead evolving them appropriately and strategically.

In short, before we take a course entirely outside the objectives of the book, Software Architecture, in my view, consists of defining the components of a software, its communication, and behavior with other software and its environment.

Something that should be done by the entire team as we usually have someone responsible for "rendering accounts" about the standards and evolution of the solution, as well as facilitating communication between teams and systems so that the solution evolves easily and adds value to the company and its customers.

I started the book with this reflection, because it is useless to study all the development patterns since the team does not talk, does not act as a team where everyone is responsible for the definition and evolution of architecture, the quality, and delivery of projects.

Now that we put some dots on the i's, let's go to the development standards.

Development Standards

There are several development standards, which are techniques/ways of organizing our code/environment, helping us to develop software with agility, quality, and that makes it easy to maintain and evolve. We usually see them in articles and books by their name: Design Patterns.

The way we use or combine these standards is defined according to the type of solution we are going to work on, what the requirements are, environment, desired experience, funds available for the project, in short. Several factors affect how we develop software.

Some standards have stricter rules and recommendations, while others do not. There is no magic recipe that will solve all problems. Therefore, the need for an experienced developer and architect, who have already lived through different situations in projects, to be able to help the team overcome challenges, which they have already lived through, or something similar, and to pass on that experience, this knowledge, forming new experienced leaders.

As stated before, the architect must closely monitor the projects in which he is involved — not just making a document or archetype in a standard repository for the company's developers - especially the newer ones, who still have a long way to go - having to guess how to evolve that without a guide.

Everyone must participate and define the evolution of the software, but the most experienced, mainly an architect, will know how to lead the team on the right path.

GoF (Gang of Four) Standards

According to the book "Design Patterns: Reusable object-oriented software solutions," "GoF" patterns are divided into three types.

But what is GoF? In 1995 a group of people, more specifically four, wrote a book starting the most well-known Design Patterns on the market: Erich Gamma, Richard Helm, Ralph Johnson, and John Vlissides. They were known as Gang of Four, or GoF.

There are countless other development patterns in addition to the book, adding up to more than 125 different patterns. But, from now on, in this book, we will cover some important standards set by GoF. The standards, according to GoF, have the following format:

- Name: an identification for the pattern

- Objective / Intent: Also known as (aka)

- Motivation: a scenario or situation showing a problem to be solved

- Applicability: How to identify scenarios where this standard is applicable

- Structure: a graphical representation of the class structure of the pattern, using a class diagram (UML), for example

- Consequences: what are the advantages and disadvantages we will have when applying the standard

- Implementations: what details should we be concerned with when implementing the standard, including for each language to which it applies

- Known uses

- Related patterns: other patterns that are similar or that can be used together for solving the problem

Given the structure that we will use to present the standards, we have 23 defined by the GoF, which have been classified into three families:

Creation Standards

- Abstract Factory

- Factory Method

- Builder

- Prototype

- Singleton

Structural Patterns

- Adapter

- Composite

- Bridge

- Decorator

- Flyweight

- Facade

- Proxy

Behavioral Patterns

- Chain of Responsibility

- Iterator

- State

- Command

- Mediator

- Strategy

- Interpreter

- Memento

- Template Method

- Observer

- Visitor

Some of these patterns apply to classes and others to objects. We'll see which ones apply to what in the detail of each one. We have some extra standards to the 23 of the GoF that I believe are important to be addressed, as they are widely used today. These are:

- Dependency Injection

- Lazy Initialization

- Lock, or Traffic Light

- Repository

Pause to Memorize

I learned that striving to stay organized and study a little bit a day is worth a lot more than studying all at once on a weekend or overnight.

For this introduction not to be too extensive, we will begin to address the detail of each pattern from the first chapter of this book. Stay tuned, as I intend to publish another book this series quickly, with a short interval between one book and another.

For now, we stop here with this inception. Let's explore the chapter one, where we will start with the advanced clean architecture pattern.

Chapter 1

The Concept of
Clean Software Architecture

Software architecture is the structure of a program or computer system that includes software components that are visible to the outside of the properties of these components, as well as the relationships between them. This term also applies to the documentation of software architecture.

Documentation of the software architecture simplifies the process of communication between stakeholders (stakeholders), allows you to capture early-stage design decisions about high-level system design, and allows you to reuse components of this design and templates in other projects.

Since its formation, the field of computer science has faced problems related to the complexity of software systems. Previously, complexity was solved by developers by properly selecting data structures, developing algorithms, and applying the concept of delimitation. Although the term "software architecture" is relatively new to the software development industry, the fundamental principles of this area have been used prominently by software pioneers since the mid-1980s.

The first attempts to understand and explain the software architecture of the system were full of inaccuracies and suffered from a lack of organization, and often it was simply a diagram of blocks connected by lines. In the 1990s, an attempt was made to identify and systematize the main aspects of the discipline.

The main idea of the discipline of software architecture is the idea of reducing the complexity of the system by abstraction and separation of powers. To date, there is still no agreement on the precise definition of the term "software architecture."

Being at the moment of its development, a discipline without clear rules about the "right" way to create a system, software architecture design is still a blend of science and art. The "art" aspect is that any commercial system implies an application or mission.

The key goals a system has described by scripts as non-functional requirements for the system are also known as quality attributes that determine how the system will behave. System quality attributes include fault tolerance, backward compatibility, extensibility, reliability, maintainability, availability, security, usability, and other qualities.

From a software architecture user perspective, software architecture provides direction for moving and solving tasks related to the specialty of each such user, such as an interested person, a software developer, a software support team, a software support specialist, a software deployment specialist, a tester, as well as end-users.

In this sense, software architecture actually integrates different perspectives on the system. The fact that these several different points of view can be combined in software architecture is an argument for protecting the need and feasibility of creating a software architecture even before the software development stage.

Architecture is the principle of organizing components within a system: their quantity, quality, interfaces, and interaction protocols.

Does that depend on the architecture? It depends on the price of support, and development of new features, labor costs for building an entire system using this architecture. That is, formally depends on the architecture of the most important parameter of development - cost. And indirectly, the possibility of reusing the code, and with it the reduction of labor costs for each further development.

Well, we found out that architecture is a very important aspect of development. But what is it? In the context of PHP5, applications focusing on the paradigm are class hierarchies, interfaces, and interaction schemes.

Choosing or creating an architecture depends on specific tasks. For example, how versatile is the application, what modules should be present, what is the scheduled load on the resource?

Therefore, any program code has interdependencies of one part from another. Classes require other classes, and some functions cause others, etc. as any interdependence project grows more and more. Project requirements change, developers sometimes make quick and not always successful decisions.

If the dependencies are not properly managed, then the project will inevitably begin to rot. The code becomes harder to understand, and it breaks down more often, becomes less flexible and difficult to reuse. As a result, the speed of development falls, the project resists change, and now the developers are calling out, "Let's do it all! Next time we will do a super-architecture." Here are the most common signs of bad or decaying project code:

- **Closure (rigid)** - the system desperately resists change, it is impossible to say how long it will take to implement one or the other functionality because changes are likely to affect many components of the system. Because of this, it becomes too expensive to make changes because they take a long time.

- **The Instability Brittle (fragile)** - the system breaks in unexpected places, even though changes were made to it, broken components clearly not affected.

- **Real Estate or Solidity (not reusable)** - based system and so the dependence is such that use any components apart from the others is not possible.

- **Viscosity (high viscosity)** - The project code is that doing something wrong is much easier than doing something right.

- **Unnecessary Repetition (high code duplication)** - the size of the project is much larger than it would be if abstraction used frequently.

- **Excessive Complexity (overcomplicated design)** - the project contains solutions that benefit from the obvious, they hide the real nature of the system, making it difficult for her understanding and development.

Almost any more or less experienced developer can recall an example of a code that matched at least one for this feature.

How to Make the Best Architecture

For many years, intelligent people have developed some fundamental principles of PLO that adhere to create a better architecture:

- **High-class code (High Cohesion)** - code responsible for anyone's functionality to be concentrated in one place.

- **Low connectivity code (Low Coupling)** - classes must have minimum dependence on other classes.

- **Indicate, but do not ask (Tell, Do not Ask)** - classes containing data and methods for handling data. Classes should not be interested in data from other classes.

- **Do not talk to strangers (Do not talk to strangers)** - Classes have to know only their immediate neighbors. The less the class knows about the existence of other classes or interfaces, the more robust the code.

All of these recommendations are intended to try to divide the classes into the sides, focus strong relationships in one place, and draw clear demarcation lines in the code.

But these principles are too vague, so there is some set of clearer rules that should be followed when designing architecture.

- **The Principle of Personal Responsibility (Single Responsibility Principle)** - a class has only one responsibility because there is only one reason that leads to change.

- **The Principle of Opening and Closing (Open-Closed Principle)** - Classes should be open for extension but closed for modification. It doesn't seem possible, but the Strategy design template is worth mentioning, and it becomes more or less clear.

- **The Principle of Substitution Liskov (Liskov Substitution Principle)** - child classes can be used via interfaces base classes without knowledge that it is the child class. Otherwise, the child class should not negate the behavior of the parent class and should be able to use the child class wherever the parent class was used.

- **Dependency Inversion Principle (Dependency Inversion Principle)** - within the system are based on abstractions. Top-level modules are independent of lower-level modules. Abstractions are independent of details.

- **The Principle of Separation of the Interface (Interface Segregation Principle)** - customers should not get dependent on the methods that they use. Customers determine what interfaces they need.

Good Architecture Principles: Open-Closed Principle (OCP)

Software entities such as classes, modules, and functions must be open for expansion but not closed for change.

You can discuss it when writing your classes to be sure that when you need to extend the behavior, you won't have to change the class, but you can extend it. The same principle applies to modules, packages, and libraries. If you have a library of multiple classes, there are many reasons why you would prefer an extension instead of changing the code already written (for backward compatibility, back to pre-testing, etc.). This is the reason we need to make sure that our modules follow the opening-closing Principle. With respect to classes, the principle of opening and closing can be guaranteed to be useful by using Abstract Classes and specific classes to implement their behavior. It will have to have Specific Classes, expanding Abstract Classes instead of changing them. Some particular cases of this principle are the Template Pattern and Strategy Pattern.

Liskov's Substitution Principle

Derived types must be able to be completely replaced by their basic types.

This principle is merely an extension of the Opening-Closing Principle in terms of behavior, which means that we must be sure that the new derived classes are an extension of the base classes without changing their behavior. New derived classes must be able to replace the base classes without any changes to the code. The Liskov Substitution Principle was introduced at the 1987 Conference on Object-Oriented Programming Systems Languages and Applications in Data abstraction and hierarchy.

Single Responsibility Principle

The class should have only one reason to change.

In this context, responsibility is seen as the only reason for the change. This principle states that if we have two reasons for changing a class, then we must divide the functionality into two classes. Each class should have only one responsibility, and in the future, if we need to make one change, we will do so in the class that holds that one responsibility. When we need to make changes to a class that has more responsibilities, the change can affect other class functionality.

Tom DeMarco introduced the Single Responsibility principle in his 1979 book Structured Analysis and Systems Specification. Robert Martin revised this concept and determined that responsibility is the cause of change.

Interface Segregation Principle

Customers should not be dependent on interfaces that they do not use.

This principle teaches us to take care of how we write our interfaces. When we write interfaces, we have to take care of adding only the methods that should be there. If we add methods that should not be there, then classes that implement the interface will need to implement unnecessary methods just like other methods. For example, if we create an interface called Worker and add the lunch break method, then all workers will have this extra method implemented. And what if the worker turned out to be a robot?

Interfaces contain methods that are not specific to them, and such methods cause the interfaces to be called dirty or greasy. We must avoid creating such interfaces.

The Principle of Dependency Inversion

(Dependency Inversion Principle) - Dependencies inside the system are based on abstractions. Top-level modules are independent of lower-level modules. Abstractions are independent of details.

This principle is very important and worthy of detailed consideration.

The Principle of Dependency Inversion in Detail

In contrast to poor design, a good architecture design should be flexible, resilient, and reusable. The lower the interoperability of the application components with each other, the greater the flexibility and mobility of the whole program as a whole. High mobility programs allow you to reuse your components over and over again to accomplish the same tasks. This reduces code duplication. Such programs consist of a large set of rather small components, each of which does a small part of the work, but does it qualitatively. Smaller components are much easier to test, implement, and maintain.

If you adhere to the principle of dependency inversion, your code is more adaptable to change and less dependent on the context of execution. The opposite is also true. If your application is a good example of successful architecture design, then it, in one way or another, adheres to the principle of dependency inversion.

Principle:

1. Top-level modules should not be dependent on lower-level modules. Both types of modules must depend on abstractions;

2. Abstraction should not depend on implementation. The implementation must depend on the abstraction.

Traditional development methods (e.g., procedural programming) tend to create code in which high-level modules are just dependent on low-level modules. This is because one of the goals of these development methods is to define a hierarchy of subroutines, and therefore a hierarchy of calls within modules (high-level modules cause low-level). This is the reason for low design flexibility and rigidity. When used properly, GO techniques allow you to work around this limitation.

Consider an example program that copies the data entered from the keyboard to a file.

We have three modules (in this case, these are functions). One module (sometimes called a service) is responsible for reading from the keyboard. The second - for output to the file. And the third high-level module combines two low-level modules to organize their work. Our copy module might look something like this.

```
while (($ data = readKeyboard ())! == false)    {    writeFile (". /
filename", $ data);  }
```

The low-level readKeyboard and writeFile modules have high flexibility. We can easily use them in a context other than the copy function. However, the copy function itself cannot be reused in another context. For example, to send data from a system log handler file.

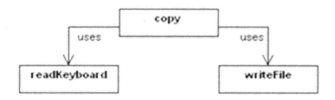

Using the dependency inversion principle, you can make the copy module independent of the source and destination objects. To do this, you must create abstractions for these objects, and make the modules dependent on these abstractions rather than on each other. interface IReader { public function read (); } interface IWriter { public function write ($ data); } The copy module should rely solely on the abstractions produced and make no assumptions about the individual features of the I / O objects. while (($ data = $ reader-> read ())! == false) {

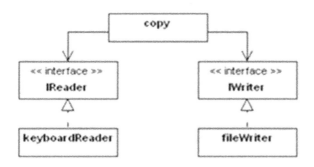

$ Writer-> write ($ data);
}
This is how a user uses our module.
$ Copier = new copier ();

21

```
// Copy keyboard data to
$ Copier-> run (new keyboardReader (), new fileWriter ('.
/ Filename'));

// Send data from file system file
processor $ Copier-> run (new fileReader ('. / Filename'),
new syslogWriter ());
```

The copy module can now be used in different copy contexts. Changing the behavior of the copier is achieved by associating it with objects of other classes (but which depend on the same abstractions).

Despite the simplicity of our actions, we have received a very important result. Now our code has the following qualities:

- the module can be used to copy data in a context different from the given one;
- we can add new I / O devices without changing the copy module.

Thus, the fragility of the code decreased, its mobility and flexibility increased.

Code Reuse

Code reuse is a methodology for designing computer and other systems, consisting of the fact that the system (computer program, program module) must consist, in whole or in part, of parts previously written into components and/or parts of another system.

Reuse is the basic methodology used to reduce labor costs when developing complex systems.

The most common cause of code reuse is application libraries. Libraries provide a generic, rather versatile functionality that covers the chosen subject area. Examples:

- Function library for complex numbers,
- Function library for 3D graphics,
- TCP / IP library,
- Database library.

New application developers can use existing libraries to solve their problems.

Reusing code outside of one project is almost impossible unless you have a framework developed. Different projects have different sets of services, which makes it difficult to reuse the object.

Designing a project frame takes a lot of effort and time. But even if, for some reason, you didn't build one, there are a few ways to encourage code reuse.

Framework Systems

What is a framework system? Why do you need it? What can she do for you? And what's wrong? In this book, I will try to answer these questions.

Internet technologies over the last ten years have taken a very big leap forward, becoming the proving ground for business and e-commerce. The development of the global network has led to the development of Internet applications. Previously, sites were nothing more than "fence announcements," now they are full-fledged programs capable of performing the tasks of automating data collection, data processing, and information provision.

Modern web developers face a very wide range of tasks. This is effective for dealing with relational databases, storing and processing XML data, building flexible information display systems, and more. This set of tasks makes old application development methods extremely inefficient. This leads to the thought of having a dedicated web developer toolkit to help him or her solve frequently occurring problems and tasks.

So, what is a framework?

When a person solves a problem many times in a row, he learns to solve it quickly and effectively! In terms of web-programming, the framework-system (CMF-system) is a platform that allows you to solve the problems that are constantly encountered when creating Internet applications. It is not necessary to think that the CMF-system is simply a set of modules for solving various tasks, which are numerous on the Internet. The framework is something more. These are:

- Terminology that allows developers to talk very concisely about complex things;

- A set of architectural standards that the system imposes on Internet applications. This eliminates the need for developers to come up with everything from scratch and allows you to reuse code more efficiently;

- Modules for solving "essentials" tasks, which allow you to start development from an empty place without inventing your own.

The web developer framework plays the same role as the toolkit with the installer tools. Even if the installer can do his job without his suitcase, he will spend more time, and the quality of the work done will be an order of magnitude lower. A similar situation is observed in the process of creating Internet applications.

CMF and CMS

Considering the concept of framework-system, we cannot avoid the concept of a content management system. Very often, the concepts of CMF (Content Management Framework) are confused with the concept of CMS (Content Management System). This is incorrect because these are fundamentally different things.

CMF systems cannot be compared to CMS systems! This is a major rule that is often broken by developers when discussing issues related to the development and use of CMF systems. CMF and CMS are different concepts, despite their similarity.

CMS is a set of modules for quick site creation. Unlike CMF, the CMS system is a complete product that is aimed primarily not at programmers but at users unfamiliar with the intricacies of creating Internet applications. The CMS system (very often called the "site engine") allows you to create a site or portal in a matter of hours that consists of a limited set of ready-made modules (news, guestbook, and forum). For the most part, CMS systems are created without further growth. The result is the absence of rigid internal system architecture. This significantly complicates the project support process.

If you have enough CMS capabilities, then most likely, you will be satisfied. However, if you are asked to change the design or extend the capabilities of the program, in most cases, you will have to resort to the help of skilled programmers. And maybe even they will not just understand this CMS-system. After reading the next paragraph, you will understand why there are so many "possible" and "most likely" in this paragraph.

The above applies to "pure" CMS-systems. That is, to CMS systems that are written from scratch on a blank. Fortunately, no one interferes with the benefits of both types of systems. Recently, CMF / CMS systems have started to appear on the Internet. These systems are a CMS system created based on the framework. The benefits are obviously determined by internal architecture, which in most cases, is documented and developed mechanisms of abstraction that do not depend on CMS-forming modules.

It is much easier to maintain a project created based on CMF / CMS-system than a project created based on a "pure" CMS-system.

This is because, in the first case, when creating a CMS-system, programmers have to fulfill several requirements dictated by the framework. Thanks to this, the CMS system has a distinct architecture,

If the CMS system is a finished product, then the CMF system is a toolkit by which you can create absolutely any product, including the CMS system. Since the framework system is a set of tools, programmers are required to use it, and they can work with these tools. This is another point that is characteristic of CMF - training staff to work with the CMF-system.

CMF system products (applications based on them) are distinguished by their individuality and high level of adaptation to the situation because they are software solutions designed to address a specific range of tasks in a specific context. With CMF, you can create any kind of online application, starting with guestbooks, ending with online shopping, and web services.

Having experts who know the architecture of the CMF system in use makes it relatively easy to extend the system, perform security audits, etc.

Architecture of CMF System

In the previous sections, much has already been said about architecture. It may seem that architectural standards are completely unnecessary. But it must be understood that such a "dictatorship" is not intended to limit the programmer's decision-making. On the contrary, it is designed to maximize the flexibility of the architecture and make it painless to change. Of course, such qualities have to be sacrificed to bring simplicity and transparency to the system.

Architectural issues are very complex, and even many experts cannot say in five minutes, anything clear about any specific decisions. But despite such a large contextual dependency of the architecture on the type of application, there are well-researched and proven options for solving architectural problems. These solutions are called Design Patterns. In one form or another, design templates can be applied to all applications. Detecting optimal implementation of templates is an integral part of working on a framework system (I would say that a true framework system is imbued with the spirit of design patterns).

Design templates exist for all major types of tasks performed by the CMF system. These tasks require thoughtful standardization (of course, within the project). There are several such tasks:

- Processing of the IP request 1);

- Organization of the subject area of IP;

- Organization of IP submission;

- Organization of auxiliary subsystems;

The tasks I have outlined are too conditional on being considered as a formal list of framework-system tasks. This list is for you to understand in which areas developers are concentrating their efforts.

Request Processing

The query processing subsystem compares the client query with the action performed by the system. Queries to the system can be quite "diverse." They differ both in appearance and semantic load. It depends on the type of application. The mapping mechanisms themselves and their actions may change during project support. These requirements dictate to the developers of the CMF-system the need to create a convenient mechanism for analyzing and processing requests. If developers do their job, then applications built on their framework will be beautiful and easily remembered by addresses like "http://www.server.com/news/2005-02-03" instead of " http: / / www.server.com/index.php?module=news&action=show&date=20 05-02-03 ». Of course, the beauty of the request is not the only quality that developers seek.

Organization of the Subject Area

Each information system has a subject area. This is a set of terms, objects, and rules that the application operates. Organization of the subject area, one of the most difficult tasks facing the developers today. In the vast majority of cases, relational databases and object-oriented display technologies provide the functioning of the subject area. The relational and object-oriented approach is brilliant separately. However, their composition, when misbehaving, turns the architecture of the information system into a pile of junk, which will be difficult to even an experienced specialist.

Organization of the Presentation

An idea is a data display subsystem. With it, the logic of the domain is separated from the logic of the data display. Imagination is the most stable part of the information system. Data display can change very often, unlike the data itself and the methods used to process it. Therefore, the framework system should provide convenient and flexible mechanisms for working with display logic. To solve this problem, we use a template system, whose task is to separate the logic of the display and compile it into separate files (display templates), which can be edited separately from all other parts of the system. Thanks to this, work on the project can be effectively paralleled (Organization of the domain → programmer + database administrator, Organization of the presentation → layout engineer + designer).

Organization of Auxiliary Subsystems

Auxiliary subsystems mean a set of architectural solutions designed to facilitate the work of the programmer. These include the implementation of general-purpose patterns that do not directly relate to other subsystems. In particular, auxiliary subsystems include such concepts as resolvers, handles, different registry (s), observers, etc. These things can be used in any other subsystem to solve emerging issues.

For example, a singleton pattern (single) can be used to support multiple instances of an object in a single instance. This task is purely auxiliary and cannot be attributed directly to the level of business logic or any other.

However, the importance of decision-making with respect to this subsystem should not be underestimated. How convenient and efficient the implementation of auxiliary patterns will depend on how convenient it is to program the other subsystems and how efficiently they will work. The code written in this subsystem largely determines the code that will be written by the programmer using this framework.

Small Libraries

One of the enemies of code reuse is the fact that people don't compile their library code. A reusable class can be buried in a directory of one of the programs and may never experience the exhilarating sense of reincarnation in a new project. And only because the programmer did not want to bring this class (or classes) to the library.

One of the reasons for the tragedy is that people do not like small libraries. There is something in small libraries that people think is wrong. Suppress this feeling. Your computer absolutely does not care how many libraries you have.

If you've written code that can be reused but doesn't fit into your library, create a new one.

Keep your Library Base [repository]

Most companies have no idea what code they have. And most programmers still do not report what they have done and are not interested in what is already written. Repositories are designed to make things better.

In an ideal world, a programmer could go to a site, look through a directory or search to find the right package of libraries, and download for himself. If you can set up a system where volunteers will support the source database, it's great. If you get a librarian who keeps track of your reuse ratio, then it's just gorgeous.

Another way is to generate source code repositories automatically. This is achieved by using standard headers for classes, methods, libraries, and various subsystems. These headings are both technical guides and items in the repository list.

Included Files

Being able to reuse existing code is very important because it can save time and money and promote consistency. Suppose a Web site contains a text menu that is repeated on each page. Instead of re-encoding the menu, it will be much easier to encode it once and dynamically include menu content on each of the individual Web pages. This can be done through the so-called server file include.

Included files can contain any XHTML or PHP code and are usually stored with the extension. Inc., although you can also use extensions Php., Txt., or. Htm. The contents of the included file are encoded once and included in any required number of PHP pages. If a change is made under the included file, the update is automatically reflected on all PHP pages that link to that file.

Below is an example of a default file that includes the title of a page.

Header.inc

<h3> Welcome to WebBooks.Com </h3>

This example shows a file that is included with the header.inc name. The file contains the text "Welcome to WebBooks.Com", surrounded by the XHTML <h3> tag. It creates a third-level header that can now be included on all the pages that make up WebBooks. After creating an included file, it can be included in the PHP page using one of the following functions:

- require (filename) - includes and validates the specified

- include file (filename) - another way of connecting files

In the following example, the header.inc file is included in the existing PHP page:

```
<? Php
   require ('header.inc');
   echo "<p> This is the WebBooks site ... </p>";
   ?>
```

The require () function calls the header.inc file and checks the contents of the file. The content is then displayed as if it were part of the home.php page. In this example, the require () function is encoded at the top of the page because it contains header information. The require () statement can, however, be included anywhere in a PHP document. The location of require () determines where the contents of a file will be displayed in the context of a PHP page.

Welcome to WebBooks.Com

This is the WebBooks site ...

It is important to note that when using included files that contain sensitive information, such as passwords or user information, the files must be stored using the extension. Php, not. Inc. or another non-standard extension. Files that use non-standard file extensions can be downloaded from the Web server, and their contents can be viewed as plain text — using the extension. Php guarantees that the client will not be able to see the source code; the server will only return the XHTML code.

Using Features

Functions are used to split large blocks of code into smaller, more manageable ones. The code contained within the function performs a specific task and returns a value. PHP contains two types of functions - user-defined (or programmer-created) and internal (built-in functions) that are part of the PHP language definition.

This section is dedicated to creating and applying specific user features.

Certain user features are created using the function keyword. They are especially useful in large PHP applications, as they may contain blocks of code that can be called or used in the program, to avoid rewriting the code. The following is an example of a simple user-defined PHP function:

```
function AddNumbers ($ num1, $ num2)
    {

        echo "This is an example of a PHP function. It calculates
    the sum of two numbers and returns the
        the result that is called in the program";

    return $ num1 + $ num2;


    }
```

Certain user functions can be called anywhere in the PHP code block. In PHP, the function is executed when used in the code of its name. After the call, the function receives all the values passed to it in the form of parameters, performs certain tasks, and returns the value caused by the program. A simple example is shown below.

```
<? Php
    function AddNumbers ($ num1, $ num2)
```

```
        {
        return $ num1 + $ num2;
        }
        echo "Sum of 5 and 2 is equal". AddNumbers (5.2);
        ?>
```

However, the AddNumbers () function defined at the beginning is only called later in the program. The function is called in the echo statement. The line "Sum of 5 and 2 is equal" is displayed. The function name connects to the output string, thus causing the function. Two parameters are passed to the function - 5 and 2. They are assigned to the function parameters of $ num1 and $ num2. The parameters are added, and the return statement is called to "return" the value or sum of two numbers to the place in the PHP code block that originally called the function. The output of the result is shown below:

The sum of 5 and 2 is 7

Function names follow the same rules as PHP variables. Valid names can begin with a letter or underline, followed by any letter, number, or underline.

Chapter 2

Design Patterns For Clean Architecture

A s the basis for the design of information, systems are used "typical solutions" or "design patterns" (Patterns).

Design patterns are many times used architectural designs that provide a solution to a general design problem within a specific context and describe the significance of the solution.

A pattern is not a completed project sample that can be directly converted to code, but rather a description or a sample of how to solve a task so that it can be used in different situations. Object-oriented templates often show relationships and interactions between classes or objects, without determining which end classes or objects the application will use. Algorithms are not considered as templates, because they solve the problem of calculation, not design.

In the 1970s, architect Christopher Alexander drew up a set of design patterns. In the field of architecture, this idea has not received such development, as later in the field of software development. According to Christopher Alexander's definition: "Each typical solution describes a recurring problem and a key to solving it, in such a way that you can use the key repeatedly, without ever having come to the same result."

In 1987, Kent Beck and Ward Cunningham took Alexander's ideas and developed templates per Smalltalk's graphical software development software.

In 1988, Eric Gamma began writing a doctoral dissertation at the University of Zurich on the general applicability of this methodology to program development.

In 1989-1991, James Coplin worked on the development of C ++ programming idioms and published in 1991 the book Advanced C ++ Idioms. In the same year, Eric Gamma completed his doctoral thesis and moved to the United States, where, in collaboration with Richard Helm, Ralph Johnson, and John Vlissides, he published the book Design Patterns - Elements of Reusable Object-Oriented Software. This book describes 23 design patterns. The team of authors of this book is also known to the public as Gang of Four (often referred to as GoF). It was this book that led to the increasing popularity of design patterns.

Another prominent figure in the field of software systems design, who has supported the use of patterns, is Martin Fowler, who wrote the book "Patterns of Enterprise Application Architecture." As Martin Fowler noted in his book, "To take advantage of typical solutions, remember that they are just a starting point, not a destination."

Craig Larman's book UML and Design Patterns describes 9 General Responsibility Assignment Software Patterns (GRASP) patterns that are used in object-oriented design to solve common class assignments and objects. Each of them helps to solve a specific problem that arises in object-oriented analysis, and that arises in almost any software development project.

The main benefit of each individual template is that it describes the solution of a whole class of abstract problems. Also, the fact that each template has its own name facilitates discussion of abstract data structures (ADTs) between developers, as they may refer to known patterns. Thus, due to the templates, the terminology, module names, and project elements are unified.

A properly formulated design template allows you to use it again and again when you find a successful solution.

However, sometimes templates preserve a cumbersome and inefficient system of concepts developed by a narrow group. As the number of templates grows beyond the critical complexity, artists begin to ignore the templates and the entire system associated with them. Often templates are replaced by the absence or shortcomings of documentation that is complex in the software environment.

It is believed that the blind application of templates from the directory, with no understanding of the reasons and prerequisites for the selection of each individual template, slows down the professional development of the programmer. People who hold this view believe that it is necessary to get acquainted with the lists of templates when "grown-up" to them in a professional plan - and not earlier. A good criterion for the required degree of professionalism is the selection of templates independently, based on your own experience. In this case, of course, familiarity with the theory associated with templates is useful at any level of professionalism and directs the development of the programmer in the right direction. Only the use of templates by reference is in doubt.

Templates can promote bad application development styles, and are often blindly applied.

The design templates are classified as follows:

Patterns of Design of Classes/Objects

- Structural patterns of design of classes/objects
  - Adapter - GoF
  - Decorator or Wrapper - GoF
  - Proxy or Surrogate GoF
  - Information Expert - GRASP
  - Composite - GoF
  - Bridge, Handle, or Body - GoF
  - Low Coupling - GRASP
  - Flyweight - GoF

- o Protected Variations - GRASP
- o Facade – GoF

- Patterns of designing class/object behavior
  - o Interpreter - GoF
  - o Iterator or Cursor - GoF
  - o Command, Action or Transaction GoF
  - o Observer, Publish-Subscribe or Delegation Event Model - GoF
  - o Don't talk to strangers (GRASP)
  - o Visitor - GoF
  - o Mediator - GoF
  - o State - GoF
  - o Strategy - GoF
  - o Memento - GoF
  - o Chain of Responsibility - GoF
  - o Template Method - GoF
  - o High Cohesion - GRASP
  - o Controller - GRASP
  - o Polymorphism - GRASP
  - o Artificial (Pure Fabrication) - GRASP
  - o Indirection - GRASP

- Generic design patterns
  - o Abstract Factory, Factory. name Toolkit (Kit) - GoF

- Singleton - GoF
- Prototype - GoF
- Creator Instances Creator - GRASP
- Builder - GoF
- Factory Method or Virtual Constructor - GoF

- Architectural system patterns / Structural patterns
  - Repository
  - Client / server
  - object-oriented, Domain Model, Table Module (Data Mapper)
  - Layers or abstract machine
  - Data flow (conveyor or filter)

- Management patterns
  - Patterns of centralized management
  - Call - Return (Transaction Scenario - Single Case)
  - Dispatcher
  - Event-based control patterns
  - Transmission of messages
  - Interrupt management
  - Patterns that interact with the database
  - Active Record
  - Unit Of Work
  - Download on Demand (Lazy Load)

- Identity Map Collection
- Record Set
- Single Table Inheritance
- Class Table Inheritance
- Optimistic Offline Lock (Optimistic Offline Lock)
- Displays with foreign keys
- Display using Association Table Mapping
- Pessimistic Offline Lock (Pessimistic Offline Lock)
- Identity Field
- Data Mapper
- Client Session State Session
- Server Session State Session
- Row Data Gateway
- Table Data Gateway
- Patterns designed to represent data on the Web
- Model View Controller
- Page Controller
- Request Controller (Front Controller)
- Template View
- Transform View
- Two-Step View
- Application Controller

- Patterns of integration of corporate information systems
    - Structural integration patterns
    - Point-to-point interaction
    - Star Interaction (Integrating Environment)
    - A mixed way of interacting
    - Patterns by integration method
    - Data-centric integration
    - Functional-centric approach
    - Object-centric
    - Integration based on a single concept-centric model
    - Integration patterns by data type
    - File sharing
    - A common database
    - Remote procedure call
    - Messaging

There are also some other templates available today:

- Carrier Rider Mapper, sharing stored information;
- analytical templates that describe the basic approach for requirement analysis prior to the start of the software development process;
- Communication templates that describe the process of communication between individual members/employees of the organization;

- organizational templates that describe the organizational hierarchy of the enterprise/firm;
- Anti-Design-Patterns describe how not to act when designing programs, showing the typical design and implementation errors;

Let's take a closer look at some of the design patterns, and patterns overview for designing classes/objects

Structural patterns include:

- Adapter - GoF;
- Decorator or Wrapper - GoF;
- Proxy or Surrogate - GoF;
- Information Expert - GRASP;
- Composite - GoF;
- Bridge, Handle, or GoF;
- Low Coupling - GRASP;
- Flyweight - GoF;
- Protected Variations - GRASP;
- Facade - GoF.

Here are examples of two of these patterns

Examples of structural patterns of classes/objects

Linker (Composite) - Go

Problem: How to treat a group or composition of object structures at the same time?

Decision: Define classes for composite and atomic objects so that they implement the same interface.

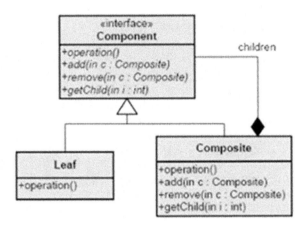

Facade - Go

Problem: How can you provide a unified interface with a set of distinct implementations or interfaces, such as a subsystem, if the high connectivity to that subsystem or the subsystem implementation may change?

Decision: Identify one point of interaction with the subsystem - a facade object that provides a common interface with the subsystem and puts the responsibility for its interaction with its components. A facade is an external object that provides a single point of entry for subsystem services. The implementation of other components of the subsystem is closed and not visible to external components. The facade object provides the implementation of the "Resistance to Change" pattern in terms of protection against changes in the implementation of the subsystem.

Behavioral patterns include:

- Interpreter - GoF;
- Iterator or Cursor - GoF;
- Command, Action or Transaction - GoF;
- Observer, Publish - Subscribe or Delegation Event Model - GoF;
- Don't talk to strangers - GRASP;
- Visitor - GoF;
- Mediator - GoF;
- State (GoF);
- Strategy - GoF;
- Memento - GoF;
- Chain of Responsibility - GoF;
- Template Method - GoF;
- High Cohesion - GRASP;
- Controller - GRASP;
- Polymorphism - GRASP;
- Pure Fabrication - GRASP;
- Indirection - GRASP.

Here are examples of three of these patterns.

Iterator or Cursor – GoF

Problem: A composite object, such as a list, must give access to its elements (objects) without revealing their internal structure, and it is necessary to sort through the list differently depending on the task.

Decision: An "Iterator" class is created that defines the interface for accessing and sorting elements, "SpecificIterator" implements the interface of the "Iterator" class and monitors the current position when bypassing the "Unit." "Aggregate" defines the interface for creating an iterator object. The "SpecificAgregator" implements the iterator creation interface and returns an instance of the "SpecificIterator" class, the "SpecificIterator" monitors the current object in the aggregate and can compute the next object when iterates.

This pattern supports various ways of sorting the unit.

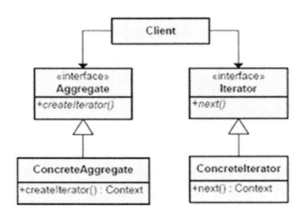

Visitor - Go

Problem: An operation is performed on each object of some structure. Define a new operation without changing object classes.

Decision: A client using this pattern must create an object of the Specific Visitor class and then visit each element of the structure. "Visitor" declares a "Visit" operation for each "SpecificElement" class (the name and signature of the operation identify the class the Visitor element is visiting - that is, the visitor can access the element directly). "Specific Visitor" implements all operations declared in the Visitor class. Each operation implements a fragment of an algorithm defined for the class of the corresponding object in the structure.

The Specific Visitor class provides the context for this algorithm and stores its local state. The Element defines an Accept operation that accepts the Visitor as an argument, and the Specific Element implements an Accept operation that accepts the Visitor as an argument. Object Structure can enumerate its arguments and provide the visitor with a high-level interface to visit their elements.

It is logical to use this pattern if there are objects in the structure of many classes with different interfaces, and it is necessary to perform operations that depend on specific classes, or if classes that establish the structure of objects rarely change, but new operations on this structure added frequently.

This pattern simplifies the addition of new operations, integrates related operations in the Visitor class.

This pattern makes it difficult to add new SpecificElement classes because you need to declare a new abstract operation in the Visitor class.

State - Go

Problem: To vary the behavior of an object depending on its internal state

Decision: The Context class delegates state-dependent queries to the current SpecificStat object (stores the instance of the SpecificStatus that defines the current state) and defines an interface of interest to clients. ConcreteStat implements behavior associated with some state of the Context object. Status defines an interface for encapsulating behavior associated with a specific instance of Context.

This pattern localizes the state-dependent behavior and divides it into parts corresponding to the states, transitions between states become apparent.

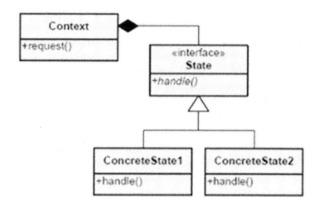

Generic Design Patterns include:

- Abstract Factory, GoF;

- Singleton - GoF;

- Prototype - GoF;

- Creator Instances Creator - GRASP;

- Builder - GoF;

- Factory Method or Virtual Constructor - GoF.

Here are examples of two of these patterns: generating patterns of classes/objects.

Singleton - Go

Problem: What special class should the Abstract Factory create, and how should it be accessed? Only one instance of the special class is required, and different objects must access that instance through a single access point.

Decision: Create a class and define a static class method that returns this single object. It is wiser to create a static instance of a special class rather than declare the required methods static since you can use an instance method to inherit and create subclasses. Static methods in programming languages are not polymorphic and do not allow overlapping in derived classes. An instance-based solution is more flexible, as it may not require a single instance of the object.

Factory Method or Virtual Constructor - Go

Problem: Define the interface to create the object, but leave the subclasses to decide which class to instantiate, that is, delegate instantiation to the subclasses.

Decision: The Creator abstract class declares a Factory Method that returns an object of type Product (an abstract class that defines the interface of objects created by the factory method). The "Creator" can also define a default Factory Method implementation that returns a "specific product." The Specific Creator replaces the Factory Method, which returns the SpecificProduct object. The "creator" "relies" on its subclasses in defining the Factory Method that returns the "SpecificProduct" object. This pattern eliminates the designer from having to embed code-dependent classes in the program. However, when applying this pattern, there is an additional level of subclasses.

The structural patterns include:

- Repository;

- Client / server;

- Object-oriented, Domain Model, Table Module (Data Mapper);

- Layers or abstract machine;

- Data flows (conveyor or filter).

Here is an example of one of these patterns: texture patterns of architecture.

Layers or Abstract Machine

Description: According to the "Multilevel system" pattern, the structural elements of the system are organized into separate levels with interconnected responsibilities so that low-level and general-purpose services are located at the lower level, and application logic level objects are located at the higher level. The interaction and linking of the levels occur from the top down. Bottom-up object binding should be avoided. The figure shows the typical levels of logical system architecture.

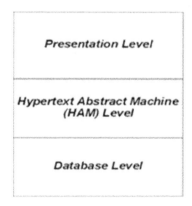

The presentation layer covers everything that is relevant to the user's communication with the system. The main functions of the view layer include displaying information and interpreting commands by the user with their transformation into appropriate operations in the context of the domain (business logic) and data source.

A data source is a subset of features that interact with third-party running systems.

Unlike the Client-Server architectural pattern, layers do not have to be placed on different machines at all.

A multilevel system can be developed step by step (Iterative).

The disadvantages of this pattern are:

- Changing the source code entails the processing of all elements of the system since all elements of the system are closely linked.

- The logic of the program is closely related to the user interface - it is difficult to change the interface or principles of logic implementation. Due to the high connectivity, it is difficult to split the system implementation work between developers and, in addition, it is difficult to modify the features of the application or to switch to new technologies.

Control patterns include:
- Patterns of centralized management

- Call - Return (Transaction Scenario - Single Case)
- Dispatcher
- Event-based control patterns
- Transmission of messages
- Interrupt management
- Patterns that interact with the database
- Active Record
- Unit Of Work
- Download on Demand (Lazy Load)
- Identity Map Collection
- Record Set
- Single Table Inheritance
- Class Table Inheritance
- Optimistic Offline Lock (Optimistic Offline Lock)
- Displays with foreign keys
- Display using Association Table Mapping
- Pessimistic Offline Lock (Pessimistic Offline Lock)
- Identity Field
- Data Mapper
- Client Session State Session
- Server Session State Session
- Row Data Gateway
- Table Data Gateway

The patterns intended for presenting data on the Web include:

- Model View Controller;
- Page Controller;
- Front Controller;
- Template View;
- Transform View;
- Two-Step View;
- Application Controller.

Here is an example of four patterns designed to represent data on the Web.

Model View Controller

A typical model-controller view involves three separate roles. A model is an object that provides some domain information. The model does not have a visual interface, and it contains all data and behavior that is not related to the user interface. In an object-oriented context, the object of the domain model is the most "pure" form of the model. A transaction script may also be considered as a model if it does not include any logic related to the user interface. Such a definition does not extend the concept of the model very much, but it fully corresponds to the role distribution in the typical solution under consideration.

The view displays the contents of the model through a graphical interface. Thus, if the model is a buyer object, the corresponding view may be a frame with a bunch of controls or an HTML page filled with buyer information. The view functions are only to display information on the screen. All changes of information are processed by the third "participant" of the system - the controller. The controller receives input from the user, performs operations on the model, and indicates the need for appropriate updates. In this respect, the GUI can be considered as a collection of views and a controller.

Talking about a typical model-controller view, there are two main types of separation: the separation of the view from the model and the separation of the controller from the view.

Model separation is one of the fundamental principles of software design. The existence of such a division is very important for several reasons:

- Representation and model belong to completely different areas of programming.

- Users want the same information to be displayed in different ways depending on the situation.

- Objects that do not have a visual interface are much easier to test than objects with an interface.

The key to separating the view from the model in the direction of dependencies: the view is model dependent, but the model is not dependent on the view. This means that changing the view does not require changing the model.

Separation of a controller from representation - A classic example of the need for this separation is to support edited and unedited behavior. This can be achieved by having one view and two controllers (for two use cases), where controllers are the strategies used by the view. Meanwhile, in practice, in most systems, only one controller is responsible for each representation, so no separation is made between them. This solution was mentioned only with the advent of Web-based interfaces, where the separation of the controller from the view was extremely useful.

Page Controller

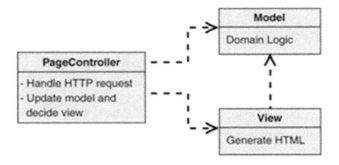

The Page Controller is based on the idea of creating components that will act as controllers for each page of the Website. In practice, the number of controllers does not always exactly match the number of pages, because sometimes clicking on links opens pages with different dynamic content. To put it more precisely, a controller is required for every action that involves a click on a button or a hyperlink.

The page controller can be implemented as a script (CGI script) or server pages (ASP, PHP, JSP, etc.). Usually, using a server page involves combining in one file the page controller and submitting a template. This is good for a template view, but not very good for a page controller since it complicates the proper structuring of this component. This problem is not so important if the page is used for a simple display of information. However, if the use of the page implies the existence of logic associated with obtaining user data or selecting a view to display the results, the server page may be populated with the code of the implemented script.

You can use a helper object to avoid such problems. When prompted, the server page invokes an auxiliary object to handle all available logic. Depending on the situation, the helper object can return control of the original server page or access another server page to act as a view. In this case, the request handler is a server page, but much of the controller logic is enclosed in the helper object.

A possible alternative to the described approach is to implement a script and controller handler. In this case, when the request is received, the web server transmits the script management; the script performs all the steps assigned to the controller and then displays the results with the desired view.

The main responsibilities of a Page Controller are listed below.

- Analyze the URL and retrieve user input into the appropriate forms to gather all the information needed to complete the action.

- Create model objects and invoke their data processing methods.

- Determine the view that should be used to display the results and provide the model with the necessary information.

The page controller does not have to be a single class, but all classes of controllers can use the same helper objects. This is especially useful if the webserver needs to have multiple handlers that perform similar tasks. In this case, using a helper object avoids duplication of code.

If necessary, some URLs can be handled by server pages and others by scripts. URLs that do not have or have almost no controller logic should be handled well by server pages because the latter is a simple mechanism that is easy to understand and make changes to. All other addresses that require more sophisticated logic require scripting.

Request Controller (Front Controller)

The Query Controller handles all requests coming to the Website and usually consists of two parts: the Web Handler and the command hierarchy. A web handler is an object that actually receives POSTs or GET requests sent to the Web server. It extracts the necessary information from the URL and the request input and then decides what action to initiate and delegates it to the appropriate team.

The web handler is usually implemented as a class, not a server page, since it does not generate any feedback. Commands are also classes, not pages of the server; moreover, they do not need to know about the presence of the Web environment, even though they are often transmitted information from HTTP requests. In most cases, the Web handler is a fairly simple program whose functions are to choose the right team.

Team selection can be static or dynamic. Static command selection involves parsing URLs and applying conditional logic, while dynamic extracting some standard URL snippets and dynamically creating an instance of a command class.

The advantages of static command selection are the use of explicit code, the availability of compile-time checks, and the high flexibility of possible URL spellings. In turn, using a dynamic approach allows you to add new commands without requiring changes to the Web handler.

When selecting commands dynamically, you can put the name of the command class directly in the URL or use a properties file that will bind URLs to the names of the command classes. Of course, this requires the creation of an additional properties file, but it will allow easy and easy change of class names without looking at all the Web pages available on the server.

Template View

The basic idea behind a typical template submission solution is to insert markers into the text of a finished static HTML page. When you call a page to service a query, these tokens will be replaced by the results of some calculations (for example, the results of queries to the database). Such a scheme allows you to create a static part of the page using conventional tools, such as WYSIWYG text editors, and does not require knowledge of programming languages. Markers refer to individual programs for dynamic information.

A variety of software tools uses a template view. Thus, the task is not so much to develop the decision itself, but rather to learn how to use it effectively and to become acquainted with possible alternatives.

Integration Patterns of Corporate Information Systems

Structural Integration

Patterns Structural integration patterns include:

- Point-to-point interaction;
- Star interaction (integrating environment);

- Mixed mode of interaction.

Patterns by Integration Method

Patterns by integration method include:

- Data-centric integration;
- Functional-centric approach;
- Object-centric;
- Integration based on a single concept-centric model.

Integration

Patterns by Type of Data Exchange Integration patterns by type of data exchange include:

- File sharing;
- General database;
- Remote procedure call;
- Messaging.

In this lecture, examples of integration patterns by type of exchange will not be considered.

Model-Viewer-Controller

The standard Model-View-Controller architecture scheme is shown in the following figure: (The scheme is borrowed from Williams's Ajax in action book)

MVC Architecture Scheme Let's look at the points in this scheme. The MVC template, as the name implies, has three main components: Model, View, and Controller. The view is responsible for displaying information coming from the system or system. The model is the "essence" of the system and is responsible for the direct algorithms, calculations, etc. of the internal structure of the system.

The controller is the link between the "view" and the "model" of the system, through which it is possible to separate between them. The controller receives the data from the user and transmits it to the "model." In addition, it receives messages from the model and transmits them to the "view."

With regard to Internet applications, it is believed that parts of the controller and views are combined, because the browser is responsible for displaying and simultaneously entering information. You can agree with this, but you can disagree and select the controller in a separate part, which we will do.

So, let's agree:

- Presentation. Output module information. It can be a template or something similar, the purpose of which is only to present information in the form of HTML based on any ready data.

- Controller. Input and output control module. This module should monitor the data transmitted to the system (via form, query-string, cookie, or any other method) and, based on the data entered, decide:

- Transmit or model them

- Display error messages and request re-input (force the module to be submitted refresh page with conditions)

In addition, the controller is obliged to determine the type of data received from the model (whether it is a ready result, no error message) and to pass the information to the view module.

Model

A module was responsible for directly calculating something based on user-generated data. The result obtained by this module must be transmitted to the controller and must not contain anything related to the direct output (i.e., it must be presented in an internal program format). It is quite difficult first to understand and understand. It takes time and a proper project. But in reality, there is nothing complicated about it.

Imagine being a representation of any class that outputs a result or error message using a template engine. Its input is either an array of data (an object or something else), or a variable containing an error text.

The controller will be the controller that performs all the necessary data validation checks and generates error messages. It is advisable to place the data validation in the controller class; they are used quite often. Alternatively, you can simply inherit a controller class from a more general class that implements validation of the input data by the specified rules. Or, if convenient, include a class or a series of data validation features in the controller class.

The same class must pass the resulting model work to the view class for output. In a word, the flow of data in this architecture is difficult to explain, so let's turn to the UML language and sequence diagram in particular (the slight deviations from the UML taken in the diagrams are that in some cases, along with entity or entity names, the data translates in parentheses).

This diagram shows the sequence of actions as well as the sequence of data transmitted: from user to user and between modules. The diagram shows the typical process of outputting a form, filling it with the user and returning the results to the user. There are no errors in this case.

Sequence Diagram

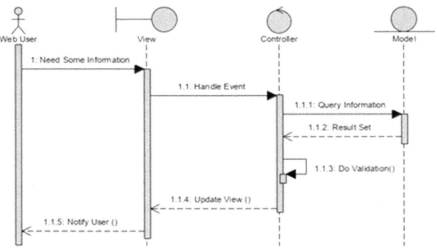

As can be seen from the diagram, the model is accessed only if the user submits the correct data. At the internal level of the application, the model is separated from the view and the controller. The controller is also separate from model and representation, and its function is to control and validate.

Now let's try to make a class diagram for clarity.

Class Diagram

The class diagram contains three classes, one for each component of the MVC architecture. For convenience, they are called: Model, View, and Controller. There are three functions in the view (though it is possible to do only one) that are responsible for displaying the status of the program: displayDefault () is the output of the default form.

displayError (error = false) - output of error message form,
displayResults () - output of calculation results

The controller has not only methods but also fields. Everything is simple with the fields: it is a mistake and the results of the calculations. By default, they are set to false, indicating that there are no errors or results yet.

The three methods present in the controller are for control and verification. The validate () method is optional and may be missing if no validation is required.

The processData () method is used to output the default form, but it also includes the userRequest method(), whose functionality only works when user input is provided. It is the userRequest () method itself that contains the validate () function (if no data is entered, so there is nothing to check), and, in addition, the model class constructor must be called.

The model can contain any number of fields and methods. However, two methods must be mandatory (or even one. As convenient as possible).

calculate () - function that produces the basic calculation
getData () - function that returns the result data.

The division of functions of the model is more meaningful. It is enough to create one method that will count and return the result.

We return to the methoduserRequest () controller. After the result has been calculated and returned in one form or another, it can be safely passed to the input of the function displayResults () of the View class. However, it should be noted that in principle, it is possible to submit an idea and an instance of a model class if the output is stored in its fields, and there are many of them (if lazy, so to speak, create a structure, an array, or any other volumetric data type).

If the controllers validate () function detects an error and sets the value of the error field to a value other than false, the controller itself will call the ViewError () method of displayError.

Now it is appropriate to give the same sequence diagram, but replacing in it the semantic values, the names of the functions of the classes in the corresponding diagram.

Sequence Diagram so, actually, we have three classes and an algorithm for interacting between them. The essence of an MVC architectural template is to divide the system view, control, and model clearly. This is very convenient because if something changes in one part of the system, the other parts will not be affected. For example, in a play, we might write: // This is a code in the PHP public function displayDefault ()

```
{
echo "<p> Enter a name:";
echo "<input type = 'text' name = 'name' value = ">";


}
```

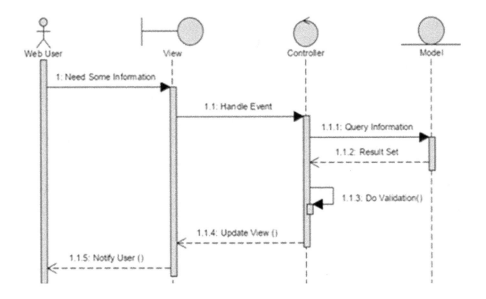

Or, for example, in the model, change a couple of calculation formulas. Either pick up a couple of restrictions in the controller or change the method of receiving and transmitting data. If you take into account the principles of inheritance in the PLO, the MVC architecture will become even more convenient. Let's say when two forms look the same but are slightly different from the calculation algorithms.

So, we got the simplest MVC system. We distinguish the positives and negatives:

The disadvantages include:

- Increase the volume of code
- The need to adhere to a predefined interface

- To support the development requires more qualified specialists

The last requirement in our example does not apply, but for real systems, it is quite relevant.

The advantages include the following:

- Certainly more flexible code
- Ability to reuse each of the three MVC components
- Painless model replacement (other calculation algorithms, storage method, etc.)
- Simply switch from one submission to another (from HTML to XML or JSON)

I must say that the example code is not perfect. It has spaces for refactoring (even though it takes up just over a hundred rows). Let's say there is only one variable coming from the user (name) in the example, but what if there are many?

Chapter 3

Clean Architectural Styles

Architectural style defines the rules for the selection of components and the organization of their interaction within the system or subsystem as a whole. Various architectural styles are suitable for various tasks in ensuring non-functional requirements - different levels of performance, ease of use, portability, and ease of maintenance. The same functionality can be implemented using a variety of styles.

Work on the isolation and classification of architectural styles was made in the mid-1990s. The results presented in the works. Below is a table of several architectural styles, highlighted in these studies.

Types of Styles	Usage Context and Key Decisions	Examples
Data Flow, Conveyor	The system outputs clearly defined output as a result of processing clearly defined input data, the processing process is time-independent, applied many	

	times, equally to any input data. The processing is organized in the form of a set (not necessarily a sequence) of individual components-processors, transmitting their results to the input of other processors or to the output of the whole system. Important features are a well-defined data structure and the ability to integrate with other systems	
Batch Processing	One single output is based on reading someone set of data at the input, and the intermediate transformations are organized in the form of a sequence	Software system build: compilation, system build, documentation build, test execution
Channels and Filters	Continuous data flows need to be transformed. The transformations are incremental, and the following can be started before the end of the previous one. There may be multiple inputs and multiple outputs. Further conversions may be added in the future.	UNIX utilities
Closed-Loop	It is necessary to ensure that incoming events are handled in a	Built-in control systems in cars,

Control	poorly anticipated environment.	aviation, satellites.Query processing on heavily loaded Web servers.
	A common event manager is used to classify an event and submit it for asynchronous processing to an event handler of this type, after which the dispatcher is again ready to accept events	Handling user actions in the GUI
Callback	The order of action is clearly defined, the individual components can't do the work without getting access from others	
Procedural Decomposition	The data is unchanged; procedures for working with them may change a little, new ones may emerge. A set of procedures is highlighted, the control transmission scheme between which is a tree with the main procedure at its root.	The basic scheme for building C, Pascal, or Ada.
Abstract Data Types	The system has a lot of data, the structure of which can change. Important opportunities for change and integration with other systems. There is a set of abstract data	Class and component libraries

	types, each of which provides a set of operations to work with that type of data. The internal view is hidden.	
Layer System	There is a natural stratification of system tasks into sets of tasks that could be solved sequentially - first, the first level tasks, then, using the solutions obtained, the second, and so on. Important portability and reusability of individual components. The components are divided into several levels so that components of this level can use only neighbors or previous level components for their work. There may be weaker restrictions, for example, upper-level components are allowed to use components of all levels below	Telecommunication protocols in the OSI model (7 levels), real protocols of data networks (usual 5 levels or less).
Client-Server	The tasks that are solved are naturally distributed between the initiators and the request handlers, the external representation of the data and the ways of their processing may be changed	Business Application Core Model: Client applications that perceive user and server requests that execute these requests

Interactive System	The need to respond quickly enough to user actions, the variability of the user interface	
Data- View-Processing (Model-View-Controller, MVC)	Changes in the external representation are likely enough, and the same information is presented differently in several places, the system must respond quickly to changes in the data. There is a set of components responsible for storing data, components responsible for their perceptions for users, and components for commands that convert data and update their perceptions.	Most often used when building applications with GUI. Document-View в MFC (Microsoft Foundation Classes) — the document in this schema combines the roles of the data and the handler
Presentation - Abstraction - Control	An interactive system based on agents with their own states and user interface, it is possible to add new agents. The difference from the previous scheme is that for each individual data set, its model, representation, and control component are combined into an agent responsible for all work with that data set. Agents only interact with one of the clearly defined parts of the control components interface	

Data Warehouse-Based Systems	The main functions of the system are related to the storage, processing, and presentation of a large amount of data	
Repository	The order of operation is determined only by the flow of external events. A shared repository is allocated. Each handler runs in response to an event corresponding to it and somehow transforms some of the data into a repository	Development environments and CASE systems
Chalkboard (blackboard)	The method of solving the problem is generally unknown or very time-consuming, but there are known methods, partially solvable tasks, the composition of which is able to produce acceptable results, it is possible to add new data consumers or processors. Separate handlers are started only if the repository data for their work is prepared. Data readiness is determined by some template system. If multiple handlers can be run, their priority system is used	Text recognition systems

Many of the styles represented are quite general and are often found in different systems. In addition, you can often find that the same system used by several architectural styles - one of the predominant ones, the other - the other, or one style is used to highlight the major subsystems, and the other - to arrange smaller components into subsystems.

More consideration should be given style "channels and filters," "Multi-System." Descriptions follow this.

Channels and Filters

Organization of processing data streams when processing breaks down into several steps. These steps can be carried out by individual handlers who may have different developers, or even organizations realized. It should take into account the following factors:

The forces acting:

- Should be possible changes in the system by adding new ways of processing and recombination available handlers, sometimes by end-users.

- Small steps of recombination for easier handling of different tasks.

- Handlers that are not adjacent have common data.

- There are various sources of input data - network connections, text files, hardware sensors message database.

- Output can be claimed in various views.

- Explicit storing intermediate results can be ineffective, creates many temporary files that can cause errors if his organization will intervene user.

- Possible use of parallelism for efficient data processing.

Decision

Every single task of data processing is divided into several small steps. The output is one step to the other input. Each step is implemented special component - Filter (filter). Filter consumes and produces data incrementally by small portions. Data filters are made between channels (pipes).

Structure

The main roles of the components within this style are filter and channel. Sometimes produce special types of filters - source (data source) and user data (data sink), which respectively produce only data or only consume them. Each stream processing consists of filters of alternating channels and starts and ends data source to consumers.

The filter receives its input data and processes them, adding the processing of their results, removing some parts, and transforming them into some other representation. Sometimes the filter itself requires input and produces output upon receipt, and sometimes it can instead respond to events coming data input and data output requirements. The filter typically consumes and produces some data portions.

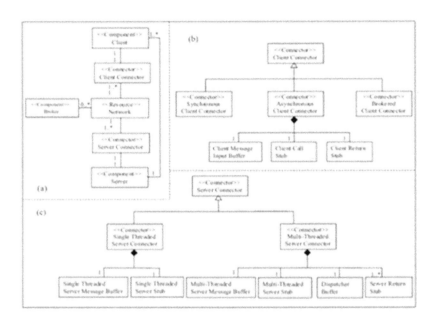

The channel provides data, their buffering and synchronization processing of neighboring filters (for example, if two adjacent active filters operate in parallel processes). If no additional buffering and synchronization is not needed, the channel may be a simple transfer of data as a parameter or result call operation.

The above figure is an example of class diagram for this sample, which sold three channels implicitly - through calls and return results of operations, and the other obviously. With filters participating in this example, the source and the consumer data, and invited Filter 1 input, Filter 3 he passes them on, and Filter 2 and invites, and transmits data independently.

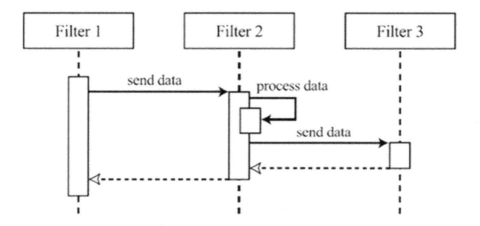

Dynamics

There are three different scenarios of one filter - push data (push model, the filter itself transmits data to the next component, and gets them only by transferring prior), extract data (pull model, the filter requires data in the previous component, the next he must demand data it) and mixed option. Often sold only one type of data for all filters within the system. In addition, the channel can buffer the synchronized data and filters interacting with it. Scenarios of the system as a whole are constructed as options for different combinations of individual filters.

Realization

The main steps are the following:

- Identify data processing steps required for solving the system. The next step is to depend on the initial data of the previous step.

- To define data formats for their transmission on each channel.

- Determine how to implement each channel, pushing or pulling data, the need for additional buffering and synchronization.

- To design and implement the necessary set of filters. Implement channels for their understanding if necessary individual components.

- To design and implement error handling. Error handling when using this style quite difficult to organize because it is often neglected. However, we need at least adequate diagnostic errors occurring at different stages.

- There may be a dedicated channel for error messages.

- In the event of mistakes entering, the appropriate filter can ignore further inputs to obtain a separator, which ensures that after reaching data unrelated to the previous ones.

- Configure the required data processing pipeline, gathering together the necessary filters and channels connecting them.

Sample Application & Consequence

Advantages:

- Intermediate data may not be stored in files but may be stored, if necessary, for any additional purposes.

- Filters can be easily replaced, overuse, rearrange, move and combine, implementing many features based on the same components.

- Conveyor system data can be developed very quickly if there is a rich set of filters.

- Active filters can work in parallel, giving a result of effective solutions on multiprocessor systems.

Disadvantages:

- Managing finish with a large general condition, which is sometimes necessary, can be realized using this style.

- Often parallel processing brings no increase in productivity since the data transmission between the filters can be expensive enough, the filters may require all incoming data before anything will be given, and their synchronization via channels can lead to significant downtime.

- Most filters spend more time conversion format input data entering their treatment. Using the same format, such as text, often reduces the effectiveness of their use.

- Error handling within this style is very complicated. In the case of the developed system must be very reliable and return to the very beginning of the work in case of mistakes, and ignoring it is not acceptable scenarios using this style is not worth it.

Examples

The most famous example of this model - a system of UNIX utilities filled opportunities shell (shell) on the organization channel between processes. Most utilities can play the role of filters in the processing of text data, and channels are built using a standard input one program with another standard output.

Another example is the commonly used compiler architecture as a sequence of filters, input machining program - lexical analyzer (lexers) parser (parser), a semantic analyzer, and generator set optimizers resulting code. This way, you can build fast enough Prototype compiler for a simple language. Productive compilers are targeting the industrial, built on the complex scheme, in particular, using elements of style "Repository."

Multi-Level System

The implementation of large systems which have a large number of diverse elements, using each other. Some aspects of these systems can include many operations performed by the various components at different levels (i.e., one problem is solved by successive applications of different levels between the elements, the other two, but involved in solving these problems elements may be different). It should take into account the following factors:

The forces acting:

- Changes in the requirements for solving one of the objectives should not lead to changes in the code of many components and should be limited to changes within a single component. The same concerns and change the platform on which the system works.

- Interfaces between components should be stable or even meet the existing standards.

- Parts of the system should be replacing. Components must be replacing other if they implement the same interfaces. Ideally may even need to progress to switch to another implementation, even if at the beginning of the system, it was not available.

- Low-level components should allow other systems to develop faster.

- Compounds with similar areas of responsibility should be grouped to improve clarity and ease of system amendment.

- It is not possible to select components of a standard size, some of them quite solve complex problems, others - quite simple. Complex components need further decomposition.

- Using a large number of components can adversely affect performance because this will often have to overcome the boundaries between the components.

- The development of the system should be effectively shared between different developers. This area of responsibility interfaces and components transmitted by different developers should be very clearly defined.

Decision

Provided a set of levels, each of which is responsible for solving its own subtasks. For this, he uses the interface provided by the previous level, providing, in turn, some interface to the next level.

Every single level can be decomposed further into smaller components.

Structure

The main components are equal. Sometimes customers are allocated using a top-level interface. Each level provides an interface to address a specific set of tasks.

Each level can be much smaller components.

Classes for conventional levels, they are usually set in smaller decomposable components

Dynamics

Scripts of the system can be obtained from these four layouts. Often sold as many levels of communication systems, two such systems can communicate through the lowest levels - in this case, a pair of symmetric scenarios (for lifting-launching applications) is performed under a common scenario on different machines.

- Appeal to the top-level client initiates a string of hits from the top level to the very bottom.

- An event at the lower level (for example, the arrival of messages on the network or clicking a mouse button) initiates a string of hits, going from the bottom to the top until some event of the top-level is visible to customers.

- Appeal to the top-level client leads to a chain of calls, which, however, does not reach the bottom. This situation is resolved, for example, if one of the levels of caches responds to queries and can give an answer earlier request that has a fed, without reference to the lower levels.

- The same can happen to the event, which is passed from the lower level. Having reached a certain level, it can be absorbed by them (with the change of status of certain components), so that it does not correspond to any event at the highest levels. For example, pressing Caps lock does not lead itself to any reactions program, but changes the value of the keys that are pressed after that, changing their case to the opposite.

Realization

The main steps are the following:

- To define the criteria for grouping task levels. This is a critical step. Improper distribution of tasks likely to lead to the need to redesign the system.

- Determine the number of levels to be implemented and their names. We often combine conceptually different tasks to achieve greater system efficiency. On the other hand, the random mixing tasks leading to fatal architecture and the system is very inconvenient for maintenance. On occasion, some put the task on several levels, which is to place it at the highest level ever, where it can be solved with sufficient performance.

- Determine the interfaces provided by the lower level of the upper. It must be remembered that a little more than the minimum necessary set of front-end operations of the lower level can achieve a significant increase in system performance as a whole.

- Identify the components and their interactions within each level.

- Identify ways of interacting adjacent levels. You can use the pushing, pulling data, or a combination of these approaches to separate the adjacent level. Ideally, the lower levels do not have to know anything about the top, and each level needs to know only the directly preceding it. For this data from the lower level can be arranged in the form callbacks (callbacks) - a pointer to a function to be called to send the message up the upper level can pass as a parameter in previous requests.

- To design and implement error handling — mistakes better handle on the lower level, which can notice them.

Sample Application & Consequences

Advantages:

- Easily replace components and overuse level one, making no impact on the rest of the levels. The ability to debug level and test separately.

- Standards support a multilevel system enables support for standard interfaces such as POSIX.

Disadvantages:

- Changing the functionality of one level can lead to cascading changes at all levels. A significant increase in performance lower level and the requirement to provide corresponding increase productivity at higher levels may also lead to a redefinition of interfaces.

- The fall in productivity due to the need to hold all calls and data through all the levels.

- Often the level of duplicating each other's work, such as handling errors as they are developed independently and have no information about the implementation details of each other.

- Many levels can lead to a significant increase in system complexity and falling productivity. On the other hand, a very small number of levels (e.g., two) often cannot provide the necessary flexibility and portability.

Examples

The most famous example of this standard - the standard model of open communication protocols (Open System Interconnection, OSI). It consists of 7 levels:

- The lowest level - physical. He is responsible for the transmission of individual bits channels. Its main task - to ensure the proper definition of zero and units in different systems to determine the temporal characteristics of transmission (for which a transmitted one bit), secure transmission in one or two directions, etc.

- The second level - or channel level data: Its mission is to provide top-level services such that the data transfer for them would look like sending and receiving a stream of bytes without loss and without overload.

- The third level – network: His task - to ensure transparent communication between computers, not conjugated directly and ensure the normal operation of large networks, which travels at the same time a lot of data packets.

- The fourth level – transport: It provides reliable data on the upper levels as some pipe - packages must arrive in the same order in which they were sent. Note that the link-layer solves the same problem, but only for machines that communicate directly with each other.

- The fifth, session layer provides an opportunity to establish a communication session (or sessions) containing a set of transmitted messages back and forth, and manage them.

- Sixth, the level of understanding defines the format of data transmitted. For example, it is determined that an integer introduced to yourself as 4 bytes, and the number of older bits coming before the younger, the first bit is interpreted as a sign, and negative numbers are represented in an additional system (i.e., 0x0000000f marks 15 and 0x80000000f - 2,147,483,633 = - (231-15)).

- Finally, the seventh level - applied - contains a set of protocols that direct use applications and users access - HTTP, FTP, SMTP, POP3, and others.

OSI model was still very difficult to use in practice. Now the most widely used set of protocols built on a stripped-down scheme OSI - it lacks the fifth and sixth level application protocol services directly using transport layer protocols.

Another example of multilevel architecture - the architecture of modern information systems or automation systems business. It includes the following levels:

- The interface of interaction with the environment.

- Often, this level is considered as the user interface, in the framework of defined views for transfer to other systems or users, a set of screens, forms, and reports which deal with users.

- Business logic, at this level, it implemented the basic rules for the operation of the business, the organization.

- Visual area. This level contains a conceptual diagram of data handled by the organization. Other organizations in their work can use these data.

- The level of resource management.

- On it are all the resources used by the system, including other systems. Often resources used are reduced to a set of databases required for the organization. The structure of resources determines this level and how to control them, in particular, specific location data to relational database tables or classes of an object database and a corresponding set of indices. Most schemes database optimized for a specific set of requests, so they look a little different from the conceptual schema of the data is the same.

Often two middle levels are combined into one - the level of performance of applications that results in the widely used three-tier architecture of information systems.

Chapter 4

Clean Architectural Design

The purpose of this chapter - to acquaint the reader with software architecture concepts and architectural design. After reading this chapter, you will:

- understand which requires architectural design software;

- Know the different models used in the documentation of system architecture;

- be aware of the different types of software architecture, structural system model, system decomposition model management model, and modular decomposition;

- Know the problem-dependent model architecture that is used as a basis for specialized software systems architecture and as a benchmark when comparing different architectures.

Large systems can always be broken down into subsystems that provide services related sets. Architectural design is called the first stage of the design process, which is defined as subsystems and management structure and communication subsystems. The aim of the architectural design is a description of software architecture.

We examined the general structure of the design process that was introduced as a model of the design process in the second chapter. The first step is to architectural design that is connecting the link between process design and process design requirements created by the system. Ideally, the specification requirements there should be information about the structure of the system. In fact, this is true only for small systems. The architectural decomposition system is necessary to structure and organize the system specification. The model system architecture is often the starting point for creating different specifications of the system. In the process of architectural design developed the basic structure of the system,

There are different approaches to the process of architectural design, which depend on professional experience and skill and intuition developers. Still, there are several steps common to all processes of architectural design.

1. **Structuring System**. The software system is structured as a set of relatively independent subsystems and also determined by the interaction between subsystems. This stage is covered in section 10.1.

2. **Modeling Management**. Developed basic model relationship management between parts of the system. This stage is covered in section 10.2.

3. **The Modular Decomposition**. Each identified in the first stage subsystem is divided into separate modules. It determined the types of modules and types of relationships. This stage is covered in the modular decomposition section.

Typically, these phases alternate and overlap. The stages are repeated for more detailed architecture processing as long as the architectural design not satisfy the system requirements.

Clear differences between the subsystems and modules not, but I think it will be following useful definitions.

1. **Subsystem**. A system (that meets the "classical" definition of "system"), operations (methods) that do not depend on the services provided by other subsystems. Subsystems are composed of modules, and interfaces are certain by which interact with other subsystems.

2. **Module**. This component provides one or more services for other modules. The module can use the services supported by the other modules. Typically, the module has never regarded as an independent system. Modules usually consist of several other, simpler components.

The result of the process of architectural design is a document that reflects the architecture of the system. It consists of a set of graphical charts. The model system with the appropriate description. The description should be specified, including a system of subsystems and modules which consist of each subsystem.

Graphical models allow the system to look at architecture from different sides. Typically, four developed architectural models.

1. The **static structural model**, which provides the subsystems or components developed further independently.

2. The **dynamic process model**, which provides the organization processes during system operation.

3. The **interface model** defines the services provided by each subsystem through a common interface.

4. **Model relations**, which shows the relationship between parts of the system, such as the flow of data between subsystems.

Several researchers, when describing the architecture of the systems, use special architecture description language. They are the major architectural elements, connectors, and components (connecting link). These languages also offer guidelines and rules for building architecture. However, like other specialized languages, they have one drawback. Namely, they are clear to experts that only mastered them, and almost never used in practice. In fact, the use of architecture description languages only complicates analysis systems. So I think that describes the architecture better uses the informal model and notation systems, such as proposed, for example, Unified Modeling Language UML.

The system architecture can be built according to certain architectural models. It is important to know these models, their weaknesses, advantages, and application possibilities. This section discusses the structural model, management model, and decomposition.

In developing the individual parts of large systems you can use a variety of architectural models. But in this case, the system architecture can be very difficult, as it will be built on a combination of different architectural models. The developer has to choose the most appropriate model and then modify it in accordance with the requirements of the developed software. Section 10.4 is considered an example of an architecture compiler model repository and a data flow model based on the combination.

The system architecture affects the performance, reliability, ease of maintenance, and other characteristics of the system because the architecture model selected for this system may depend on non-functional system requirements.

1. **Productivity**. If the requirement is critical, system performance should develop such architecture that for all critical operations answered fewer subsystems with the greatest little interaction between them. To reduce the interaction between the components, better use large modular components, not small structural elements.

2. **Multi-Layered Security**. In this case, the architecture should be multi-layered structure in which the most critical

system components are protected internally, and check the safety of these levels is carried out at a higher level.

3. **Security**. In this case, it is necessary to design the architecture so that all operations that affect system security comply with fewer subsystems. This approach allows us to reduce development costs and solves the problem of checking reliability.

4. **Reliability**. In this case, the architecture design to include redundant components so that you can replace and update them without interrupting system operation — the architecture of fault-tolerant systems with high capacity for work covered in section 18.

5. **Ease of Maintenance**. In this case, the system architecture should be designed at the level of small structural components that can be easily changed. Programs that provide data must be separated from the applications that use the data. It should also avoid sharing data structure.

Obviously, some of these architectural phases contradict each other. For example, to improve performance, you should use large modular components at the same time support system is much easier if it consists of small structural components. If you take into account both the requirements, you should seek a compromise solution. We have already mentioned that one way to solve such problems is to use various architectural models for different parts of the system.

Structuring Systems

The first phase of the design process system architecture is divided into several interacting subsystems. At the most, the abstract level system architecture can be represented graphically using a flowchart in which individual subsystems are separate blocks. If the subsystem can also be divided into several parts in the diagram of these rectangles depicted inside large blocks. Streams of data and/or control flow between the subsystems indicated by arrows. This flowchart gives an overview of the structure of the system.

The block model architecture for a system of automatic packaging various types of objects. It consists of several parts. Subsystem surveillance studies objects on the line determine the type of object and choose the appropriate type for a package. Then the objects are removed from the conveyor, packed and placed on another conveyor. Examples of other architecture shown in chapter 2.

Bess (Bass) believes that these flowcharts are useless representations of system architecture, because they cannot find anything either about the nature of relationships between system components or their properties. In terms of software developers, it's absolutely true. However, such models are effective at the stage of the preliminary design of the system. This model is not overloaded with details, with it convenient to present the structure of the system. In the structural model by all major subsystems that can be developed independently from other subsystems; therefore, the project manager can allocate the development of these subsystems between performers. Of course, understanding the architecture is not only flowcharts, but such systems represent no less useful than another architectural model.

Of course, you can develop a more detailed model of the structure, which would show how subsystems share data and interact with each other. This section discusses the three standard models, namely model repository, model client/server model, and abstract machines.

Model Repository

To subsystems, components of the system work more efficiently between them should go to the exchange of information. The exchange can be arranged in two ways.

1. All shared data is stored in a central database accessible to all subsystems. Model systems based on the joint application database, often called a model repository.

2. Each subsystem has its own database. Interchange of data between subsystems is through communication.

Most systems, machining large amounts of data organized around shared database or repository. Therefore, this model is suitable for applications in which data is created in the same subsystem, and used in another. Examples include management information systems, automatic design, and the CASE tool.

It is believed that the first CASE-funds shared repository was developed in the early 1970s British company ICL in the creation of its operating system. Widely known, this model has gained since been used to support the development of systems written in Ada, since many CASE tools developed using a common repository.

Shareable repositories have both advantages and disadvantages.

1. Obviously, sharing large amounts of data efficiently because they do not need to transfer data from one subsystem to the other.

2. On the other hand, the subsystem must be consistent with the model repository database. This always leads to the need to compromise between the requirements that apply to each subsystem. A compromise solution might reduce their productivity. If new data formats subsystems do not fit the model of coordinated views integrate these subsystems is difficult or impossible.

3. A subsystem, which generated data, do not know how this data is used in other subsystems.

4. Because, according to the agreed data model generated large volumes of information, the modernization of such systems is problematic. The translation system to a new data model is expensive and complicated and sometimes even impossible.

5. In repository systems with tools such as backup, security, access control, and data recovery, centralized as in the system management repository. These tools perform only their basic operations and do not deal with other issues.

6. On the other hand, the various subsystems imposed different requirements regarding security, data recovery, and backup. The model repository for all subsystems applies the same policy.

7. Model sharing repository clear if the new subsystem is compatible with a consistent data model; they can be directly integrated into the system.

8. However, difficult place repositories on multiple machines, as there can be problems associated with redundancy and data integrity violation.

In this model, the repository is passive element management and laid them on the subsystem using data from the repository. For artificial intelligence, systems developed an alternative approach, and it is based on the model of "workspace" that initiates the subsystem when specific data are available. This approach is applicable to systems in which data is a well-structured form.

Client / Server Model

Model client/server architecture - a model of a distributed system, which shows the distribution of data and processes between multiple processors. The model includes three basic components.

1. A set of independent servers that provide services to other subsystems, for example, print server, which provides printing, file servers, which provide services file management and server compiler, which offers services to compile the source code of programs.

2. A set of customers, causing services provided by servers. In the context of the clients are conventional subsystems — nonparallel execution of multiple instances of the client program.

3. The network helps customers get access to services. In principle, there is no prohibition to ensure that clients and servers on a single machine launched. In practice, however, the client/server model in such a situation is not in use.

Customers should know the names of the available servers and services that they provide. At the same time, the servers do not need to know any names of clients or their numbers. Customers get access to services, a service provided by means of the remote procedure call.

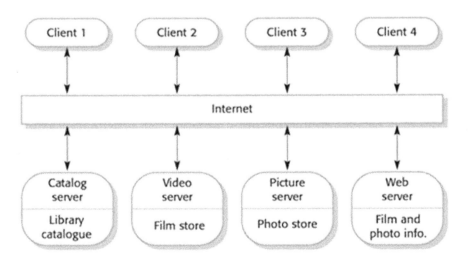

It can be organized by type of client/server model, etc. This multiuser hypertext system designed to support libraries and movies. It contains multiple servers that host different types of media files and manage them. To transfer video files quickly and simultaneously, but with a relatively low resolution, they can be stored in a compressed state, while photos must be transmitted in a high resolution. The approach of the client/server can be used in the implementation of systems based on the repository, which is supported by the server system. Subsystems that have access to the repository are customers. But usually, each subsystem manages its own data. When the server and client communicate, but the exchange of large volumes of data can be problems associated with network bandwidth. However, with the development of increasingly fast networks, this problem is losing its value.

The most important advantage of the client/server model is that it is a distributed architecture. It is effectively used in network systems with multiple distributed processors. The system is easy to add a new server and integrate it with the rest of the system or recover servers without affecting other parts of the system. Section 11 discusses distributed systems architecture details.

Abstract Machine Model

The architecture of abstract machines (sometimes called multilevel model) models the interaction of subsystems. It organizes the system as a set of levels, each of which offers its services. Each level defines an abstract machine whose machine language (services provided level) is used to implement the next level of abstract machines. For example, the most common way to implement the programming language is to determine the ideal "machine language" and compile programs written in this language, the code of the machine.

The next step is broadcast abstract machine code is converted into real machine code.

A well-known example of such a campaign can serve as a model OSI network protocols. Another example is the three-tier model of environmental programming in Ada.

*   OSI (Open System Interconnection - Open Systems Interconnection) - International standardization of data exchange between computer systems based protocols Seven model data in open systems. The model proposed by the International Organization for Standardization ISO (International Standards Organization). -Comm. Ed.*

System Administration versions based on version control facilities and provides tools for a complete configuration management system. To maintain configuration management tools used by system administration objects that support the database and facility management services. In turn, the system databases are supported by various services, such as transaction management, rollback ago, recovery, and access control for database management tools used by the underlying operating system and its file system.

The multi-step approach provides systems development - the development of services provided by him are available to users. In addition, this architecture is easily tolerated and shift to different platforms; the interface at any level will provide only the adjacent level. Since the multi-machine systems depending on the platform located at the domestic level, such a system can be implemented on other platforms because of the need to change only the domestic level.

The disadvantage of a layered approach is a fairly complex structure of the system. Fixed assets, such as file management, necessary for all abstract machines, are provided internally. Therefore, the service, the invited user may need access to internal levels of abstract machines. This situation leads to the destruction of the model as an external level depends not only on the level preceding it but from lower levels.

Managing

The model shows the structure of all the subsystems of which it is composed. To operate the subsystem as a whole, need to manage them. The structural model is not (and should not be) any information management. However, the developer must organize subsystem architecture according to some models of governance that complement the existing model would structure. In models of management-level architecture designed flow control between subsystems.

There are two basic types of control in software systems.

1. Centralized management. One of the subsystems fully responsible for the management, launching and shutting down other subsystems. Management first subsystem can

switch to another subsystem, but then must be returned to the first.

2. Management based on events. Here, instead of one subsystem responsible for the management, external events can match any subsystem. Events that are responsive system may occur either in other subsystems or in the external environment of the system.

Management Framework complements the structural model. All structural models described earlier can be implemented using centralized management or management based on events.

Centralized Management

The model of centralized management of one of the designated main and manages other subsystems. These models can be divided into two classes, depending on the series or parallel execution implemented managed subsystems.

1. Model-call return. This is a known model of program procedures call from above "down" in which management starts at the top of the hierarchy of procedures, and a call is transferred to a lower level of the hierarchy. This model is applicable only in sequential systems.

2. Model Manager. It is used in parallel systems. One system component is assigned a controller and controls the start, completion, and coordination of other system processes. The process (runtime subsystem or module) can proceed in

parallel with other processes. A model of this type is applicable also in serial systems where the application that manages individual subsystem is based on the values of some state variables. Normal control is realized through a service case.

The call-return model is presented in the figure below. From the main program can call routines 1, 2, and 3, the sub 1 - routines 1.1 and 1.2, the sub 3 - routines 3.1 and 3.2, etc. These model execution routines are not structural - routine 1.1 is not necessarily part of the subroutine 1.

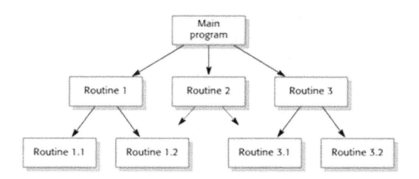

This model is integrated into the programming language Ada, Pascal, and C. Management transferred from the program, located at the top level of the hierarchy to a lower level routine. Then returns control to the point of calling routine. The management is responsible and routine that is performed in the present moment, or it may cause other routines or return control subroutine that caused it. The imperfection of programming style when returning to a certain point in the program is obvious.

The call-return model can be used in a module for management functions and objects. Routines in the programming language are called from other routines are naturally functional. However, in many object-oriented systems, operations objects (methods) are implemented as procedures or functions. For example, the Java object invites service with another object by calling the appropriate method.

The rigid and limited nature of the call-return models is both advantages and disadvantages. Advantages models are relatively simple analysis flow management, as well as choosing a system that is responsible for specific input. Lack of models is a complicated processing exception.

The next model is the model of centralized management for parallel systems. This model is often used as "soft" real-time systems that do not have too strict restrictions. The central controller controls the execution of many processes associated with sensors and actuators.

The controller system, depending on the variables of the system, determines the time to start or complete the process. It checks whether generated in other processes information to process it later or pass other processes for processing. Typically, the controller is constantly checking sensors and other processes or tracking state changes, so this model is sometimes called a model of feedback.

Systems Managed Events

In a centralized management model, typically control system determined by the values of some variable condition. In contrast to existing systems, such models managed based on external events. In this context, the event is meant not only a binary signal of "yes-no." This signal can take a range of values. The difference between the event and the conventional inputs is planning events that go beyond process control, manufacturing events. For event processing subsystem requires access to state information, but this information is not usually determined by flow control.

We have developed many different types of event-driven systems. These include spreadsheets, which change the value in any cell changes the contents of other cells, artificial intelligence, which under certain conditions there are initiating actions or objects using active, then when you change some action triggers the property value of the object. This section describes two models of managed events.

1. Models of communication. In these models, the transfer event is a message to all subsystems. Any subsystem that handles this event corresponds to it.

2. Models drove interrupts. Such models are commonly used in real-time systems where external interrupt register interrupt handlers, and other system components are processed.

Models of communication are effective at integrating subsystems distributed across networked computers. Models driven interrupts are used in real-time with strict temporal requirements.

The model of communication (Figure below) subsystem reacts to certain events. If there was some event, control passes to the subsystem manufacturing this event. Between the messaging model and centralized management model, there is a difference: the control algorithm is not built into the handler of messages and events. Subsystems determine which events need handler messages.

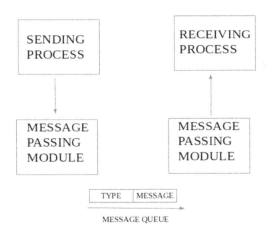

All events can generate messages of all subsystems, but significantly increases the load in the data processing. Often the event handler and manages communications subsystems register and events to which they respond. Subsystems generate events that may have data to process. Handler registers the event because of its register and transmits this event to those subsystems that react to it.

The event handler has always supported two-point interaction. Therefore, the subsystem can clearly send a message to other subsystems. There are many varieties of this model. Broker's query objects also support this management model, the interaction between distributed objects.

The advantage of the model of communication is relatively simple to upgrade a system constructed according to this model. The new subsystem can be integrated into the system of registering an event handler events. Each subsystem can activate any other subsystem without knowing its name or location. Subsystems can also be implemented on different machines.

The disadvantage of this model is that subsystems are unknown when they finish the event. The generating event subsystem does not know what kind of system will react to it. It allowed a situation where various subsystems react to the same event. This can lead to conflicts in obtaining access to the results of processing events.

Real-Time Systems, which is a requirement of fast processing of external events, should be event-driven. For example, a real-time system that controls the vehicle safety system must determine a possible accident and have time to fill air pillow safety to the head of the driver will strike the steering wheel. To ensure quick response to events, you must use management based on interrupt.

The next figure shows a management model based on interruption. Each type has its own interrupt handler. Each type of interruption associated with a memory cell, which stores the address of the interrupt handler. When a particular hardware interrupt switch immediately transfers control to the interrupt handler. In response to an event caused by the interrupt handler can start or complete other processes.

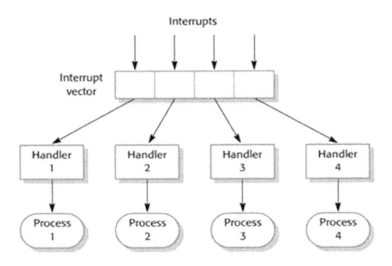

This model is only used in hard real-time systems that require an immediate reaction to certain events. You can combine this model with the model of centralized management. The central controller handles the normal progress of the system, as used in critical situations management based on interrupt.

The advantage of this approach is the immediate response to system events, drawbacks - the complexity of programming and certification systems. Almost impossible to simulate all interrupts during system testing. It is difficult to change the system, based on models such as the number of interruptions limited equipment. No other types of events are not processed when the threshold is reached. Restrictions can sometimes be circumvented if one interruption identifies several types of events and to provide for separate processing handler. However, if you need a fast response to interrupts, this approach is impractical.

The Modular Decomposition

After the development phase of the system structure in the design phase followed by the decomposition of subsystems in the module. Between the breakdown of the system into subsystems and subsystem modules are no fundamental differences. At this point, you can use the model discussed in section 10.1. However, conventional components modules subsystems fewer components, so you can use special model decomposition.

It addresses two models used during decomposition module subsystems.

1. Object-oriented model. The system consists of a set of interacting objects.

2. Model data streams. The system consists of functional modules that receive data at the input and transform them in some way to the original data. This approach is often called the conveyor.

In the object-oriented model, modules are objects with their own specific conditions and operations over these states. The model data streams modules perform the functional conversion. In both models, the modules implemented or as successive components or both processes.

If possible, developers should not make hasty decisions about whether parallel or serial system. Designing a coherent system has several advantages: sequential program easy to design, implement, test, and test the parallel system where it is very difficult to formalize, manage and verify the timing relationship between processes. It is better to first break the system into modules, and the stage of deciding how to organize their implementation - in series or parallel.

Object Model

Object-oriented architectural model structures the system as a set of weakly coupled objects with well-defined interfaces.

An object-oriented architectural model for a system of processing invoices can be created. The system issues a credit customer, receives payments, sending receipts for payments that were received, and the message to unpaid bills. In this example, the notation system used modeling language UML, in which classes of objects have names and a set of attributes. The operations if they are defined in the bottom of the rectangle indicating the object. Barcodes arrow means that objects using properties or services provided by other objects.

At the stage of object-oriented decomposition defined classes of objects, their properties, and operations, in implementing the system of these classes create objects; to coordinate the operations of facilities used any management model. In this particular example, the abacus class has various related operations (methods) that implement the functionality of the system. This class uses other classes representing customers, payments, and receipts.

The advantages of the object-oriented approach are well known. Since objects weakly linked, you can change the implementation of a particular object without affecting the rest of the objects. The structure of the system is easy to understand because objects are often the objects of the real world. For the direct implementation of the system, components can use object-oriented programming language.

However, the object-oriented approach has drawbacks. When using services, facilities must explicitly invoke the names of other objects and know their interface if you change the system to change the interface necessary to evaluate the effect of such changes based on user variables object — many real-world objects represented as a difficult system object.

Models of Data Flow

In a controlled data flow model, data passes through a sequence of transformations. Each processing step is implemented as a conversion. These systems arriving at the entrance, go through all the transformations, and reach the exit system. The transformation can be performed sequentially or in parallel. Data processing can be batch or element by element.

If the conversion presented as separate processes, this model is sometimes called the conveyor belt or filter model, following the terminology adopted in the system UNIX. Last supporting belts that act as a repository of information and a set of commands that are functional transformation. Here, the term "filter" as converting "filter" data when processing the data stream.

Different versions of the model data streams emerged with the advent of the first computers designed for automated data processing. When the conversion is treated packets of data sequentially, this architectural model called a sequential batch model. It is the basis for many classes of data. Examples are the system (e.g., processing system accounts) that generate a large number of initial reports received by simple calculations, but with more input records.

Note that this model is only part of the processing system of accounts - discharge accounts using other transformations. Compare this model with object-oriented discussed in the previous section. More abstract object model because it does not contain information on the steps. This architecture has several advantages.

1. The ability to re-use changes.

2. Clarity, as well as most people, think in terms of incoming and outgoing data.

3. The ability to modify the system by directly adding new transformations.

4. Easy to implement a consistent and parallel system.

The principal disadvantage of the model, associated with the need to use some common format of data that must be recognized by all transformations, and each conversion should coordinate with related transformations on the format of data to be processed or should be offered standard format for all data to be processed. Each conversion must comply with parse input and output data to synthesize an appropriate manner, and the computational load on the system increases. Unable to integrate transformation using incompatible data formats.

The interactive system is difficult to describe using the model data streams due to the lack of a predictable stream of data being processed although a plain text input and output can be simulated by the model data streams graphical user interfaces with complex formats and input-output management based on various events (such as a mouse click or menu selection) translated it into a form compatible with the model data streams is quite challenging.

Problem-Dependent Architecture

Considered earlier architectural model is generalized. They are widely used for many classes of applications. Along with the basic models used architectural model specific to the visual field of application. These models are called problem-dependent architecture. There are two types of problem-dependent architectural models.

1. Class model systems display classes of real systems, absorbing the main characteristics of these classes. Typically, the architectural model classes occur in real-time systems, such as data collection, monitoring, etc.

2. Basic models. Abstract developers and provide information on the general structure of a type of system.

Of course, clear differences between these types of models there. In some cases, class models serve as a baseline. Here I spend the difference between them because the basic model can be directly reused in the project. Base models are commonly used in communications systems and the comparison of the possible system architecture. Various processes and develop these models. The class model developed as a generalization of existing systems "from the bottom up," while the development of basic models is from above "down."

Models of Classes

Model Compiler is probably the most famous example of the architectural model class. At present, developed thousands of compilers. It is believed that the compiler should include modules listed below.

1. The lexical analyzer that translates the input language in some internal code.

2. Table IDs issued by the lexical analyzer, which contains information used in the program names and types.

3. Parser that checks the syntax of a compiled code. It uses the specified language grammar and creates a parse tree.

4. Parse tree that represents the internal structure of a compiled program.

5. Semantic Analyzer, which verifies semantic correctness of programs on the basis of information received from the parse tree and table identifiers.

6. Code generator that runs on the parse tree and generates machine code.

The compiler may be other components that convert the parse tree, increase efficiency, and eliminate redundancy of machine codes generated.

The components that make up the compiler can organize according to different architectural models. You can use dataflow architecture, which serves as a table identifier repository of shared data. Several steps including lexical, syntactic, and semantic analysis are performed sequentially.

This model is still widely used. It is effective where programs are compiled and executed without user intervention, i.e., in batches. However, such models are less effective when integrated with other compiler language means, such as editing system structures, interactive debugger, training of printed documents, etc.

There are currently a relatively small number of problem-dependent models of class systems. Organizations that develop similar models consider them as valuable intellectual property, as they are the basis for software development. Such models are often a series of architecture software. For example, all printer drivers, regardless of the specific printer properties, can be used the same original architecture.

Basic Architecture

The architectural model of classes reflects the architecture of existing systems. In contrast, basic models usually appear as a result of research in a specific subject domain application. They are the architecture of the idealized, which reflects the peculiarities inherent to systems operating in this visual field.

An example of the basic architecture can serve as a model OSI, which is a standard open systems interconnection. If some system is compatible with this model, it can interact with any other systems that support this standard. Thus, the system control range of goods in the supermarket, developed based on the model of OSI, can directly exchange data with the system vendor orders also developed based on this model.

On the other hand, the basic model is usually not considered as a method of implementation. Their main purpose - to serve as a benchmark for comparison of different systems in any subject domain; that is, the base model is the standard when evaluating different systems.

The next figure shows that the Seven OSI model is a model of open systems. The exact purpose of the various layers is not essential. We note only that provide lower levels of physical interaction, average levels - data, and the upper level – the transfer of semantically meaningful information, such as standardized documents, etc.

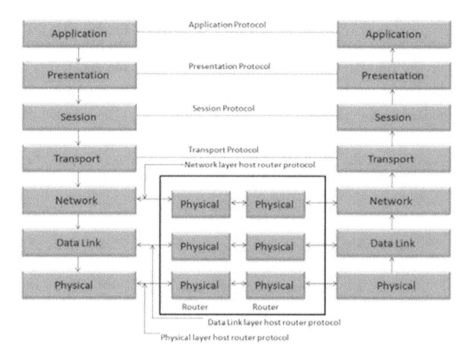

Before developers, the OSI model was set a specific goal - a standard on which would be carried interaction between incompatible systems. Each level would depend only on the level that lay below. With the development of technology in any of the levels could be implemented again, without affecting other system levels.

In practice, a multi-level approach to architectural design is a compromise. If the difference between computer networks is very large, simple interaction between them impossible. Although the functional characteristics of each level are clearly defined, remain uncertain non-functional characteristics of the system.

Therefore, developers implementing their own means of high level can "skip" some level model. In other words, to improve system performance, developers can design custom products that do not fit into the framework model. After this simple replacement levels in this model is hardly possible. However, the effectiveness of this model is not reduced. This model provides a framework for structuring the overall system and implementing interactions between systems.

Chapter 5

Clean Architecture For Six Sigma And DFSS

Six Sigma and DFSS

Motorola initiated the concept of implementing the six sigma methodology in the 1980s to reduce quality costs. The six sigma methodology has evolved from statistically oriented methods to improvements in the quality of processes, products, or services. This is a business improvement strategy used to improve profitability, to avoid expenses in the business process, and to improve the efficiency of all operations that meet or exceed customer needs and expectations. A six sigma performance level equals 3.4 defects per million opportunities, where sigma is a statistical measure of the level of variation in a process. The average level of variation for many companies is three sigmas, equivalent to 66 800 defects per million opportunities.

According to organizations that have adopted the principles and concepts of the six-sigma methodology have noted that once they reach a five-sigma level, the product life cycle is costly to them. If a design error is detected during the manufacturing stage, it will cost a hundred times more to repair than if the same error is repaired at the design stage. For which DFSS was created and among its most important benefits are:

- Reduces time to market for products

- Reduces life cycle costs associated with products

- Is focused on understanding customer expectations and priorities

- Reduces the number of design changes

Design for Six Sigma

As in Software Engineering, manufacturing companies have a customer-oriented design, where there is a transformation between the needs of the customer and the design of the solution. This process is transferred over several phases, starting from the conceptual phase where you conceive, evaluate and select a good design that provides a solution to the client's needs, which on many occasions, is not an easy task and has enormous consequences. Manufacturing and design companies usually operate in two ways:

- Fire prevention - Conceives viable and robust conceptual entities; this method is preventive.

- Firefighting - Solves design entity problems. Unfortunately, the latter consumes human resources, not human resources and time, since this method is not preventive but corrective.

The latest trends in design research are presented in two senses:

a) Improve the performance of designs according to the environment in which they are used. This robust design method was suggested by G.Taguchi (1994), in which the objective is to have a robust solution to satisfy the functional objectives and can be fulfilled through the design process.

b) The second has to do with conceptual methods, which are suggested by Suh (1990). Suh's interest has to do with design vulnerabilities that are introduced into the design solution when certain principles are violated. Suh proposes the use of axioms, and both are created to improve the design process to improve design solutions.

What is Six Sigma Design?

The main objective of DFSS is to "design right the first time" to avoid bad and costly experiences. The term six sigma in the context of DFSS can be defined as the level at which design vulnerabilities are minimal. Generally, two aspects of design vulnerability that can affect design quality are:

• Conceptual vulnerabilities that are established when design principles and axioms are violated.

• Operational vulnerabilities due to lack of robustness in the use of the environment, the elimination or reduction of these types of vulnerabilities are the objective of the quality initiatives included in Six Sigma.

The implementation of DFSS in the conceptual phase is the main goal and can be achieved by following a design methodology, combined with quality concepts and upfront methods to attack both conceptual and operational vulnerabilities.

DFSS integrates tools to eliminate or reduce these vulnerabilities, but in general, the main problem is that current design methods are empirical. They represent the best of the design community, which unfortunately lacks a scientific basis. Therefore, when companies suffer from customer dissatisfaction, experience and judgment may not be sufficient to obtain an optimal solution, and DFSS precisely addresses this problem from the early stages of design, motivating the fact that design decisions made in early stages have a great impact on the total cost and quality of the system.

The area of manufacturing research, including product development, is currently making efforts to reduce development and manufacturing costs, reduce Life Cycle Cost (LCC) and improve the quality of design entities in the form of products, services or processes. In the experience of at least 80% of the quality of the design is compromised in the early stages.

Six Sigma Design Phases

DFSS has the following four phases:

1. Identification of requirements

2. Characterization of the design

3. Design Optimization

4. Design Verification

Phase 1. Identification of Requirements

DFSS projects can be categorized as an entity design or entity redesign. "Creative Design" is the term we will use to indicate new designs and incremental designs for redesigns.

Step 1: Establish the status of the project (project charter) - Establish the duration of the project, which are generally long and with high initial costs. The duration of long projects is because the company is redesigning or designing different entities, not patching an existing design. The high initial costs are because there are many customer requirements to be identified and studied since all critical metrics that satisfy these requirements (CTS) need to be identified to conceive and optimize better designs. It also establishes the work team with both internal and external representatives (customers and suppliers), establishing roles, responsibilities, and necessary resources.

Step 2: Identify business and customer requirements - In this step, customers are fully identified and their needs collected and analyzed, with the help of the QFD tool, and Kano analysis. Then the most appropriate set of CTS metrics are determined and ordered to measure and evaluate the design (QFT and Kano analysis also help to establish limits and numerical targets for CTSs).

In summary, the following list of steps lists the steps that are followed in this phase:

- Identify methods to meet client needs.

- Obtain customer needs and transform them into a VOC (voice of customer) list.

- Translate the VOC list into functional and measurable requirements.

- Finalize the requirements:

    o Establishing the definition of minimum requirements.

    o Identify and fill the gaps in the requirements provided by the client.

    o Validate the application and environment of use.

- Identify CTSs as Critical to Quality (CTQ), Critical to Delivery (CTD), Critical to Cost (CTC), and so on.

- Quantify CTSs

    - Establish metrics for CTSs

    - Establish acceptable window performance and performance levels

Tools used in this phase - Tools used in this phase include:

- Market and customer research

- QFD

- Kano Analysis

- Risk analysis

Phase 2. Characterization of the Design

Step 1: Translate customer requirements (CTSs) into product and process functional requirements - Customer requirements, CTSs give ideas of what will satisfy the customer, but these do not ask to be used directly as the requirements for a product or process design. Customer requirements need to be translated into functional requirements. QFD can be used to add this transformation.

Step 2: Generate design alternatives - After resolution of the functional requirements for the new design entity (product, service, or process), it is necessary to characterize (design) the design entities that will be available to satisfy the functional requirements. In general, there are two possibilities:

- The existence of known technology or design concepts available to satisfy all requirements satisfactorily. So this step becomes almost a trivial exercise.

- Existing technology or design concepts are not available to satisfy all requirements satisfactorily, so new design concepts must be developed. This new design can be creative or incremental, so the TRIZ method could help generate innovative design concepts at that step.

Step 3: Evaluate the design alternatives - Several design alternatives can be generated in the previous step; therefore, it is necessary to evaluate them and make the decision of which concept will be used. Several methods can be used in design assessment, including Pugh concept selection techniques, design reviews, design vulnerability analysis, and FMEA. After the evaluation, a concept will be selected. During the evaluation, many weaknesses of the initial set of the design concept will be exposed and concepts will be revised and improved. If we are designing a process, process management exhibited techniques will be used as evaluation tools.

Tools used in this phase - Tools used in this phase include:

- TRIZ

- QFD

- Robust design

- DFMEA and PFMEA

- Design review

- CAD/CAE

- Simulation

- Process Management

Phase 3. Optimization of the Design

The result of this phase is the optimization of design entities with all requirements released at a six sigma performance level. As the design concept is finalized, some parameters can be adjusted and changed. Tools such as simulators and/or hardware testers may be useful in this phase. Usually, in DFSS, this parameter optimization phase is followed by a tolerance optimization step. The objective is to provide a logical and objective basis for configuring manufacturing tolerances.

Tools used in this phase - Tools used in this phase include:

- Design and simulation tools

- Design of experiments

- Taguchi method, parameter design, and tolerance design

- Design based on reliability

- Robust evaluation

Phase 4. Validation of the Design

After the tolerance and parameter design is completed, the validation and verification activities are executed.

Step 1: Pilot test and refinement - No product or service should go directly to the market without first being piloted and refined. In this step, DFMEA can be used as a small-scale pilot implementation to test and evaluate real-life performance.

Step 2: Validation and process control - In this step, the new entity is validated to ensure that the final result was designed knowing the design requirements and that the process control in manufacturing and production is established to ensure the critical characteristics.

Step 3: Commercial presentation and delivery of the new process to the customer because the design entity is validated, and process control is in place, the large-scale commercial launch of the new entity takes place.

Tools used in this phase - Tools used in this phase include:

- Capacity Process Modeling

- DOE

- Reliability Testing

- Confidentiality analysis

- Process control

Clean Software Architecture Processes for DFSS

In this section, we will briefly describe some of the software architecture processes that were analyzed and compared with the DFSS process to know if the process defined in DFSS was useful for Software Architectures.

Method of Design Based on Architectures

This section briefly describes the ABD method "Architecture Based Design," which provides a structure for producing the conceptual architecture of a system. Conceptual architecture is one of the four different architectures identified by Hofmeister, Nord, and Soni. This architecture describes the system in terms of the highest level design elements and the relationships between them.

The ABD method depends on determining the architectural drivers of a system, where these drivers are a combination of business, functional, and quality requirements.

The ABD method can be is broken down into conceptual subsystems and one or more software templates. At the next level, conceptual subsystems are broken down into conceptual components and one or more software templates.

This method is recursive; the steps that apply to the system are the same steps that apply to the conceptual subsystems. This method uses the term design element to refer generically to the system, a subsystem, or a conceptual component. A design element will implement a collection of responsibilities and have a conceptual interface that encapsulates the knowledge of the input and output data. The ABD method ends once decisions have been made about classes, methods, processes, and operating system threads.

Summarizing this method, we can say that it consists of the following steps: The decomposition of the system, Selection of an architectural style, Refining templates, and Verification of scenarios.

Development Based on Architectures

According to Bass and Kazman, in the development of software, architecture is a critical step in the development of critical systems. Therefore in 1999, they proposed a process for the development of software architectures called "Architecture-Based Development." The steps of this process are:

- This step generates a list of:

    a) Functional requirements (use cases)

    b) Specific architectural requirements and

    c) Quality Scenarios.

- Architectural Design - This design phase is expressed in architectural views such as:

    a) Functional

    b) Code

    c) Concurrence

    d) Physics and

    e) Development

- Architecture Documentation - Designed to serve as a basis and support for programmers and analysts. In this phase, the authors give a series of recommendations to generate maintainable documentation.

- Architecture Analysis - Evaluates the architecture to identify potential risks and verify the quality requirements that have been taken into account in the design. This evaluation is done using the ATAM method.

- Generation of the architecture - Codification of the architecture from the generated design.

- Architecture maintenance - In this phase, a series of recommendations are given to have a maintainable architecture, since they consider that it is a risk not to have the architecture documented and consistent with the design decisions.

Software Architecture Process

According to Bredemeyer Consulting, the software architecture process is divided into the following steps:

- **Start/Commit** - In this phase, the work team is formed, the team is aligned with the vision and purpose of the architecture, and the project plan is developed.

- **Architectural requirements** - Architectural requirements are established and documented.

- **System Structuring** - The purpose of this phase is to design the system at a high level and to specify architectural guidelines for designers.

- **Architecture validation** - In this phase, it is validated that the architecture knows the requirements and identifies issues and areas for improvement.

- **Deployment of the architecture** - Ensures that the architecture is being followed in the design products and the system.

Description of the Problem

One of the critical aspects of the design and construction of a complex software system is its architecture. Currently, the design process of software architecture is not fully formalized and is often more intuitive than systematic. It was not until 1990 that the term "Software Architecture" began to gain acceptance in both the research community and the industry. Professionals in architecture design have noticed that the design and development of a good architecture is a critical success factor and began to recognize the value in making decisions about the architectural style, design patterns, frameworks, etc., which will be used for the development of new products.

Some of the most critical problems that have faced software architects and that have been the subject of study of researchers are:

- The processes of software architectures are not defined in a detailed way and are not in continuous improvement.

- Perhaps the most complex activity during application development is the transformation of the requirements specification into system implementation. Although it should be noted that although this discipline of Software Engineering Requirements has also been a subject of study, this paper will use the specification of requirements as input to the design of the architecture.

- Quality requirements (RQs) strongly influence the software architecture, and these are generally treated with an informal process during the design of the architecture. Since the main focus is on the functional requirements of the system, not much attention is paid to quality requirements.

- The evaluation of architecture is another critical factor, which has not been given the value it represents, because systems are designed and implemented without an explicit evaluation, and only then are tests performed to determine whether quality requirements have been met. And if the system does not comply with them, then it is redesigned.

- Documentation is another issue to which software architects should put special interest because the documentation of the system structure and its properties has advantages for the maintenance of the system. And as we have seen and read in some case studies, a lot of time is wasted trying to understand the system code. But we know that not only the maintenance of software is benefited since many times the documentation is not effective in communicating essential information to the stakeholders of a system that is in its development stage, but many of the problems of ineffective communication also have to do with the informal notation used by software system architects. For this, some progress has been made in the use of, e.g., UML, OCL, etc.

- The existence of methods that decouple the implementation of code from the architecture, which allows inconsistencies, violate architectural properties, and inhibit the evolution of the software architecture.

- The description of the architecture in a formal way, through the ADL's.

Finally, and despite the progress that has emerged in the field of software architecture, this field still remains immature. Therefore, this paper aims to initiate an investigation in this discipline of Software Engineering along with a mixture of Six Sigma methodology called DFSS.

Chapter 6

Proposal for an Architectural Solution

This section describes the proposed solution for the process of DFSS-based software architectures called DFSS. This is based on the DFSS process and the different contributions described in the previous section.

DFSS is a process of software architectures that allows creating a new architecture, from the architectural requirements of the same one. The steps that the process presents. The steps that the process presents, which are shown in the Figure below.

1. Identification of architectural requirements

2. Characterization of the design of the Architecture

3. Architecture Documentation

4. Optimize the design of the Architecture

5. Validation of the design of the Architecture

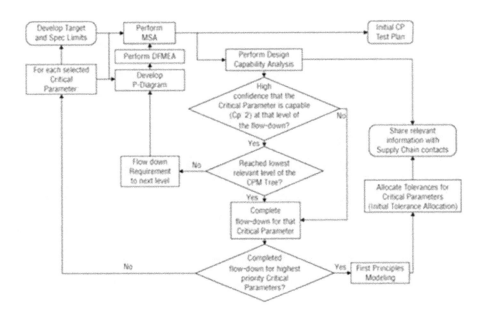

The figure above shows the general model of the proposed solution for the software architecture process. Where, as can be seen, there is the requirements stage, which has as its main objectives the creation of the work team, the selection of the methods that will be used for the elicitation of requirements, the obtaining of the same, the translation of the requirements into functional requirements and measurable quality attributes and finally the categorization of the requirements.

In the stage of Characterization of the design of the Architecture, the main objective is the creation of design alternatives, that is to say, the creation of design entities and their relations, with the objective that they fulfill the functional requirements and quality attributes. Within this phase is immersed one of the steps of great importance: the evaluation of architecture, which as we know the main objective of this stage is to verify that the architecture of the proposed software is complying with the functional and quality requirements or if there is a conflict between them that is preventing the combination of them.

The documentation stage aims to represent the prose architecture, using standard notation and a standard template according to ANSI/IEEE 1471-2000.

For the stage of optimization of the Architecture design, the main objective is based on the evaluation of the same one in the previous point - to be able to make the necessary readjustments in the design and to be able to contemplate in a greater measure all the attributes of quality.

Finally, in the validation stage whose objective is to validate that the architecture is in accordance with the requirements established by the stakeholders and in this stage, we have a double-flow with the optimization stage, this is because once the architecture is validated, it can undergo changes, so it must go through the steps defined in the mentioned stage.

The following section will describe in detail each of the stages of the DFSS process following the following guidelines: the inputs, outputs, and internal steps of each of the stages of the process will be described. A standard notation will be followed for the necessary diagrams at each stage as well as for their explanation.

Clean Process for the Development of Software Architectures Based on DFSS

The model proposed in this paper is based on the processes described in the previous section and specifically in and also takes as a reference to the model developed by Bill Smith. The six sigma or DFSS design also conforms to the defined stages.

Regarding the relationship between DFSS and Kazman and Bass' Architectural-based development process in the Figure below, we can see that the process contains the following steps:

a) obtaining architectural requirements,

b) designing software architecture,

c) documenting software architecture,

d) analyzing software architecture,

e) generating the software architecture and finally

f) maintaining software architecture.

This process coincides with the process that we are proposing DFSS in the first four steps, since the fifth step, which is the generation of the coding of the architecture, was outside the scope of this project, although it should be noted that some progress has been made and can be verified. As for step six, maintenance of the architecture was not taken into account in our model because DFSS focuses on the design of new products and/or services, and therefore is not defined, but we consider that if it is a necessary phase within the process, as we know all systems will have changes or improvements. See Figure below.

As for the improvements proposed in DFSS is that a validation stage of the architecture is added, which has the objective of being able to validate that the design of the software architecture meets the needs and expectations of all stakeholders, another of the phases that were added is the optimization of the architecture, whose objective is to make the necessary adjustments or adjustments once the verification of the architecture has been done. And finally one of the steps of the stage of Characterization of the design of the architecture is to make an analysis of risks, where the risks are analyzed the quality attributes of the architecture, as well as their possible mitigation and contingency plans in the event of any of them being presented.

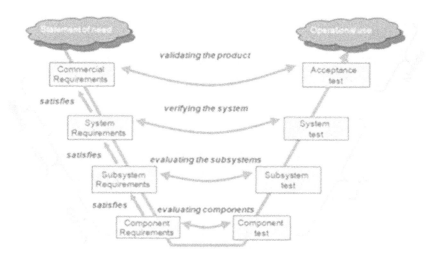

As for the relationship between DFSS and the DFSS process we can see in the Figure below, that we really have a very close relationship in the stages proposed by DFSS although it should be noted that the name of the first stage was changed from "Identify" to "Architectural Requirements" because it is a more appropriate name in the context of software architectures. As for the other stages were really respected, although it should be noted that a stage was added called architecture documentation because as was said in the section of the problem, there is currently in Software Engineering in the area of Software Architectures a serious problem as far as documentation is concerned; therefore DFSS like the processes defined in the previous section include it.

As can be seen in the next Figure, the stages of the processes are almost the same, what is adequate are the steps in each of them, as well as some of the tools, which in some cases have already been adapted to Software and others will remain pending such adaptation. This project aims to be the backbone of a process of software architectures based on DFSS since it is considered that one of the advantages is that some as have found applying DFSS that is a process that is already defined and that not only tells you the steps to follow in each of the stages but also proposes the use of tools that in some cases have been adapted to Software and that in my opinion are very helpful, although the main problem is that few software engineers put into practice the researches and proposals they make, therefore the immaturity that one has in this field of Software Engineering will be eradicated if they put into practice what is researched.

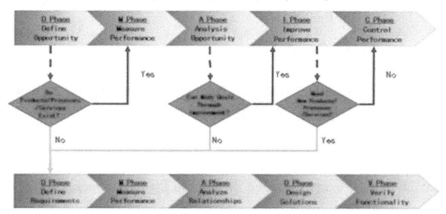

Process Six Sigma (DMAIC) – For Improving Existing Process

Design for Six Sigma (DMADV) for Designing New Product

In this way and as explained above, the DFSS model takes the best to specify its phases, adding steps that are considered important, and that will make the process more complete.

The following sections will describe each of the stages proposed in the DFSS model by taking into account the following guidelines:

- The notation for modeling the process steps is aligned to those proposed by Ericsson and Penker.

- The entrance artifacts to each one of the stages of the process will be considered.

- The internal steps in each of the stages of the process

- Output artifacts from the process stages

- Mention is made of the possible tools that will support the stages of the process.

Architectural Requirements

The main objectives of this stage are the creation of the work team, the selection of the methods that will be used for the elicitation of requirements, the obtaining of the same, the translation of the requirements to functional requirements, and measurable quality attributes and finally the categorization of the requirements.

Within this stage, some sub-stages will follow the same documentation standard mentioned in the previous section. The steps to follow in the Architectural Requirements stage are as follows:

Step 1: Start

The beginning step has to do with the creation of the work team for the design of the Architecture, as well as the creation of the project charter and the Project Plan. The act of constitution of the project or Project charter, "is the document that formally authorizes a project. This document gives the project manager the authority to apply the project resources organization to the project activities."

The project plan should be a general plan indicating the main milestones of the project.

The activities to follow from this step are:

- Acquisition of sponsorship (if applicable).

- Verification of the existence of human, non-human, monetary (if applicable) and training resources necessary for the design of the Architecture.

- To form and align the work team with the vision and purpose of Architecture.

- Establish:

  o The main objectives of the Architecture

  o The Scope of Architecture

  o The acceptance criteria of Architecture

  o The Assumptions of Architecture

  o And finally, the initial risks associated with Architecture

- Creation of the Architectural project plan

The following table summarizes step number one: Start, of the Architectural Requirements stage:

Element	Description
Tickets	- Contract - SOW (Statement of work). - Work team (personnel). - Business strategy and objectives.

| Outputs | • Architecture work plan. |
| | • Teamwork (roles and responsibilities). |
	• Project Charter.
Tools and/or techniques	• Project management and planning.
	• PM BOOK
	• Graphics by Gantt, Pert
	• TSP (Creation of work teams, roles, and responsibilities, creation of work plan)
Roles	• Analyst.
	• Architect.

Step 2: Identification of business and customer requirements

The step of identifying business and customer requirements aims to identify the main stakeholders of the project, their needs, and analyze those needs.

The activities to follow in this step are:

- Identify methods to meet clients' needs and wishes

- Identification of the main clients

- Obtain customer needs (known as WHATs in DFSS) and wishes based on functional requirements and quality attributes

- Identify customer satisfaction attributes, and each attribute is ranked according to its relative importance to the customer.

- Transform customer needs and wishes into a voice of customer list (VOC) through the SQFD tool.

- Identify CTSs in critical-to-quality (CTQ), critical-to-delivery (CTD), and so on.

CTS (critical-to-satisfaction) is an arrangement of design features derived from the responses of the WHATs. The arrangement of CTSs is also called the HOWs arrangement. Each initial WHAT must have one or more HOWs describing how to achieve customer satisfaction. For example, if the customer wants a "nice car," this can be achieved taking into account the design of the seats, the space that will be available for the legs, a car without noise, without vibrations, etc. All these are customer requirements that must be measured and controlled and are what we know as quality characteristics, which in the case of Software Architectures, requirements such as modifiability, performance, portability, etc., are quality attributes that can be obtained via the SQFD tool. See the Figure below.

The relationships between technical CTS and the arrangement of WHATs are often used to prioritize the needs and desires of customers that were embodied in the QFD matrix. Because the work team assigns a value that reflects the scope for which the STS defined contributes to knowing the WHATs.

With the steps mentioned above, it has been described how to obtain the architectural requirements using the SQFD software quality house. The software architect must specify the quality attributes in a standard way, and for this, we recommend using the ISO 9126-1 standard.

The next step and referring to the process defined by Bill Smith in the step of specifying direct and indirect scenarios, is to describe the behavior of the architecture based on quality scenarios (direct and indirect) where the direct scenarios are short statements that describe the normal use that the direct and indirect scenarios make of the architecture.

End users give the system built based on the software architecture; indirect scenarios are statements that represent changes to the architecture according to the use of new hardware or software platforms, replace any existing functionality or a component.

Scenarios are actions related to stakeholders and their interests in the system, which are based on quality attributes.

Having the scenarios we can ensure that the architecture covers the requirements, but as we know we have several stakeholders interested differently in the attributes of the system, so Kazman, Carrier, and Woods, propose the use of a three-dimensional matrix that relates the scenarios with the stakeholders and quality attributes. See the Figure below.

The following table summarizes step two: Identification of business and customer requirements from the Architectural Requirements stage:

Element	Description
Tickets	• Needs and wishes of the client's customer (Document requirements)
Outputs	• Quality Houses • Quality Scenarios • Scenario Relationship Matrix • Quality requirements

Tools and/or techniques		o SQFD
		o Market/Customer Research
		o Risk analysis
		o Methods for collection of requirements:
		o Interviews
		o Questionnaires
		o Prototypes
		o Observation
	• Kano Analysis	
	• Analytical methods (monotonic rate, concurrency, etc.)	
Roles	• Analyst.	
	• Architect.	

Characterization of the Design of the Architecture

The main objectives of the architecture characterization stage are the design of architectural design alternatives based on the client's quality requirements and attributes, as well as the verification of said architecture.

Step 1: Architecture Design

This step has to objective the design of the software architecture based on the requirements of the client; for this, it will make use of the ABD method, which provides a simple and powerful structure.

The activities to follow in this step are:

- Scenario review, scenario relationship matrix, and quality attributes.

- From the highest level of the system, break down into conceptual subsystems trying to identify architectural styles and architectural and design patterns that may be useful.

- At the subsystem level, to decompose in conceptual components or modules with specific responsibilities, at this level, also architectural patterns will be identified.

- Once the decomposition has been done, and the level of conceptual components has been reached, it will be possible to decompose concrete components that represent the design elements in architecture.

- Design elements should have a specific responsibility and be conceptualized through styles, patterns, and rules that will be determined by quality requirements and attributes.

- Once the functionality of the system has been decomposed, the architectural styles in which the architecture will be based will be selected, as well as their adaptation to the needs of the architecture.

- They will be assigned based on the decomposition of the system, the components that will be implemented (some) styles — identifying the interfaces of each of the components.

- Identification and selection of architectural patterns for a defined set of design elements.

- At a lower level of decomposition, design patterns can be identified that can be useful and adapted to specific needs.

- It is worth mentioning that based on the scenarios generated in the previous phase, it will be possible to generate more than one candidate architecture, with which the step of the evaluation will determine which architecture is the adequate one.

- Identify the architectural views that will form part of the architectural design.

- Documentation of system decomposition and decisions made.

The views that will form part of the architecture design and part of the documentation are based on those proposed by ANSI/IEEE 1471-2000, which provides guidance for selecting the largest set of views to document that supports the interests of stakeholders. This standard describes a set of views to satisfy the stakeholder community. A view identifies the set of interests to be focused on. This is a representation of a set of software elements, their properties, and the relationships between them — the choice of a set of views showing the complete architecture and all of the relevant properties.

Architectural views can be divided into three main groups, known as view types. Depending on the nature of the elements they show, these groups can be:

- *Module view type.* In this group of views, the elements are modules, which are code units that implement a set of responsibilities. A module can be a class, a collection of classes, a layer, or any decomposition of the coding unit. Each module has a collection of properties assigned to it, and these try to express the important information associated with the module, for example, its restrictions. Modules can have relationships with other modules through relationships such as: "is part of" or "inherits from." Some of the architectural styles contained in this category are: decomposition, uses, generalization, and layered.

- *Component-and-connector view type.* Styles in this type of view express runtime behavior. These are described in terms of components and connectors. Where a component is one of the main processing units of Systems execution, a connector is a mechanism of interaction between the components. Objects, processes, or collection of objects can be components, and connectors include pipes, repositories, sockets, etc. Middleware can be seen as a connector between the components that use it. Some of the architectural styles contained in this category are Pipe and Filters, shared data, publish&subscribe, client-server, peer to peer, and communicating processes.

- *Allocation view type.* This group of views shows the relationships between the software elements and the elements in one or more external environments in which the software architecture is created and executed (hardware, system files, development team, etc.). Some of the architectural styles contained in this category are deployment, implementation, and work assignment.

The following table summarizes step number one: Architecture design, from the Characterization stage of the Architecture design.

Element	*Description*
Tickets	<ul><li>Quality Scenarios</li><li>Scenario Relationship Matrix</li></ul>
Outputs	<ul><li>Architectural design</li><li>Architecture Views</li></ul>
Tools and/or techniques	<ul><li>TRIZ</li><li>QFD</li><li>Axiomatic Design</li><li>Robust Design</li><li>Simulation</li><li>DFMEA</li></ul>

	• Architectural Styles
	• Design Patterns
Roles	• Architect.

Step 2: Evaluate design alternatives

The objective of the stage of evaluation of the alternatives to the design of architectures is to be able to verify that this design fulfills the defined requirements of quality.

The activities to follow in this step are:

- Define the objective of the evaluation.

- The selection of the evaluation method based on the quality attributes to be analyzed.

- Selection of analytical methods to verify compliance with quality attributes.

- Follow the steps of the evaluation of the Architecture.

- Generation of an evaluation report.

At this stage, we can take into account the recommendation and evaluate the architecture based on scenarios, since based on their experience, the evolution based on scenarios is very useful, although it should be mentioned that Simulation, mathematical modeling and/or objective reasoning may be alternatives in the evaluation.

The following table summarizes step number two: Evaluation of the Architecture, of the stage of Characterization of the design of the Architecture.

Element	Description
Tickets	• Indirect • Direct • Architecture • eDesign • Venuese
Outputs	• Architecture Evaluation • Proposals for improvements
Tools and/or techniques	• Design Reviews • ATAM • SAAM • ABAS • SNA
Roles	• Architect

Architecture Documentation

The documentation of the architecture is one of the stages that has been neglected by software architects, but experience has shown us that it is fundamental because it serves us as a means of communication between stakeholders and the work team, translates in a textual and graphic way the design and decisions taken for it, as well as the analytical analyses carried out for the verification of quality attributes, etc. See Figure below.

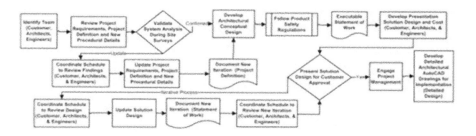

Some of the recommendations from this stage that we took are:

- The documentation must be navigable and complete.

- Design assumptions and constraints that were defined by the customer must be specified.

- Documentation must be available to all stakeholders.

The activities to follow in this step are:

- Choose the template that will serve as the basis for documenting the architecture; in this case, we make the recommendation to use the ANSI/IEEE 1471- 2000 template.

- To fill in the template following the proposed indications, here it is necessary to point out that it is not necessary to fill in all the points of the template, only those that are necessary and relevant to the consideration of the architect.

161

The following table summarizes the Architectural Documentation stage:

Element	Description
Tickets	• Architecture design, direct and indirect scenarios, and architectural views
Outputs	• Software Architectures Document
Tools and/or techniques	• ANXI/IEEE 1471-2000 • UML
Roles	• Architect • Documentation

Architectural Design Optimization

The optimization of the Architecture allows us to carry out the necessary adaptations to the design of the Architecture. See the Figure below.

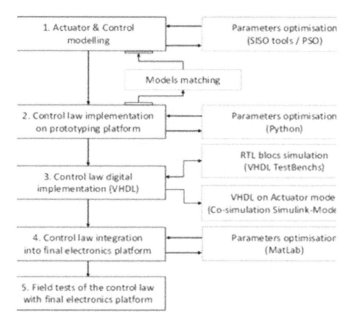

The activities to follow in this stage are:

- Based on the evaluation made and the report generated in it, define:

    o Scenarios not contemplated that may lead to changes in the design of the Architecture.

    o Requirements (functional as quality attributes) not covered in the design of the Software Architecture.

    o Identification of new requirements

- The work team, together with the Software Architect, will analyze the issues of the previous step to make the necessary modifications to the proposed design or make a new evaluation if the design is considered robust enough to support the issues detected. The analysis should take into account:

- o Changes, modifications, or additions to selected architectural styles and design patterns.

- o Assign new functionality to added or modified architectural styles and design patterns.

- o Add new components or modules

- o Make the necessary changes to the architectural views.

- o Go to the evaluation step to verify compliance with requirements (both existing and new)

- Document the changes made

The optimization of the Architecture allows us to carry out the necessary adaptations to the design of the Architecture.

The following table summarizes the Architectural Optimization stage:

Element	Description
Tickets	<ul><li>Architecture Design</li><li>Architecture Evaluation</li></ul>

Outputs	• Document of Software Architectures adapted to the recommendations that arose in the evaluation.
Tools and/or techniques	• FMEA • Simulation
Roles	• Architect

Validation of the Design of the Architecture

In this way and as explained above, the DFSS model takes the best to specify its phases, adding steps that are considered important, and that will make the process more complete.

The activities to follow in this stage are:

- Preparation of the presentation of the Software Architecture

- Presentation of the Software Architecture and the results of the evaluation, as well as the improvements and adjustments made to it.

- Generation of observations and/or requests for change

- Generation of the final report of the validation of the Software Architecture

- If the client indicates that everything is correct:

  o Liberation Delivery of Software Architecture

- Otherwise:

  o The release does not take place

The following table summarizes the Architectural Documentation stage:

Element	Description
Tickets	- Architectural Document (with improvements proposed in the evaluation, if applicable), results of the evaluation.
Outputs	- Release Software Architectures Document - Unreleased software architectures document with a change request
Tools and/or techniques	- Walk-through - Inspections
Roles	- Architect - Stakeholders

Conclusion

One of the most important elements to provide gains in agility, efficiency, maintenance and evolution of information systems is the software architecture, however, as the systems become bigger, the use of principles must be highlighted to obtain advantages in return and investment considering deadlines and final costs, with that the software architecture has entered the scene to deal with these large and complex systems. Thus, algorithms and data structures are no longer the most critical point of the construction project of the Information system. Over the past decade, software architecture has received increasing attention as an important area of software engineering.

Professionals have realized that architecture is a critical success factor for information systems; however, despite this progress, software architecture remains relatively immature.

In the article "Software Architecture: a Roadmap," by David Garlan (2000), he describes some of the important trends in software architecture in research and practice, so I bring you a summary of some of these issues.

The Role of Software Architecture

Software architecture can play an important role in at least six aspects of software development.

Understanding: Architecture simplifies the ability to understand large systems, presenting a level of abstraction in which a high-level design system can be easily understood.

Reuse: Software reuse has long been identified as a major time-saving factor. Thus, developers of another project can benefit from reusing their code, instead of reinventing it.

Construction: An architecture description provides a partial model for development through the main components and dependencies between them.

Evolution: When the software reaches a development stage considered satisfactory for a given user of the system, it may not be satisfactory for all users, even if the group of developers abandons the project at some point, nothing prevents other developers from continuing the development in a parallel version or even assume the administration of the original.

Analysis: Proper architecture provides new opportunities for analysis and constraints imposed by the style of the architecture.

Management: Projects where appropriate software architecture is used leads to a much clearer understanding of needs, implementation strategies, and risks.

The software architect should have a focus on the implications that organizational objectives will have on technical options, that is, a global view of the system. You should build models for the problem at hand, seeking to find a solution and always looking for alternative approaches, and documentation is essential to present and discuss with the other members of the development team and with the manager responsible for the project.

Past

The origin of software architecture was first identified in the research by Edsger Dijkstra in 1968 and David Parnas in the early 1970s. These scientists emphasized the importance of the structures of a software system and the importance of identifying its structure.

Years ago, architectures were largely ad hoc, and these architectures were rarely maintained once the system had been built, as people began to understand the key role that architectural design plays in determining the success of the system, they also started recognizing the need for a more organized approach. The first authors began to observe certain principles in projects to call architecture as an important field in development and to establish a working standard for software architects.

Gift

Currently, mobile technology is among the most promising in the market, the need to integrate with other platforms and devices, the constant growth in processing capacity and a wide need for applications with more complex requirements on the part of users, are just a few factors that increase the difficulty in development.

However, few proposals have been defined focusing on the specific characteristics of this area and this platform. This development, in the great majority, is still done by techniques coming from other platforms, often inadequate. Although there is not much variation, in general, the architecture is much more visible as an important activity in software development. A lot has changed in the last decade, besides the technological basis for the software architecture to have improved dramatically.

Product Lines and Standards

One of these trends has been the desire to exploit frequency in various products, with this a new approach to software reuse has motivated developers and this approach is known as Software Product Lines which is based on the reuse of software artifacts where they are established under the same architecture. This new concept has been used by developers to reduce costs and increase their productivity, but this adoption has risks that must be evaluated before starting this type of reuse.

The projects that made use of software reuse showed that without proper planning, the costs of the project with reuse could be much higher than to develop the artifacts from scratch. Thus, it is essential to plan in advance the products for which reuse will be applied. Without a doubt, the organization can obtain considerable benefits in terms of cost reduction and time to market, increase product quality, applying the development of product lines.

Coding and Disclosure

An early impediment to the emergence of software architecture as a discipline of software engineering was the lack of a shared set of knowledge about architectures and techniques to develop good results.

While recognizing the value of stylistic uniformity, software construction realities often force one to compose systems from parts that have not been uniformly engineered.

For example, you can combine a database from one vendor, with middleware from another, and a one-third user interface. In such cases, the parties do not always work well together largely because they make conflicting assumptions about the environments in which they were designed to work. This led to the recognition of the need to identify architectural strategies to avoid problems.

Future

Although software architecture today is a much more solid foundation than it was a decade ago, it is not yet established as a discipline that is universally taught and practiced throughout the software industry. One reason for this is simply that it takes time for new approaches, another reason is that the technological basis for architectural design is still immature, but the trend in the area's natural evolution is to bring continuous advances.

However, the world of software development and the contexts in which the software is being used is changing in significant ways. These changes promise to have a major impact on how software architecture is practiced, and they are considered three of the most prominent trends and their implications for the field of software architecture.

Buy or Develop?
While buying software means adapting business processes to software, developing means building an application that meets a specific process.

In fact, many companies are quickly finding themselves more in the position of system integrators than software developers. That is, most of the code they do is to write "copy and paste" code. There are several consequences for software architecture, and this trend increases the need for the entire industry.

This trend is evident in the growing popularity of 'component-based' software development. When choosing components that agree on a common architecture framework, such as JavaBeans, or CORBA, many of the problems of architecture and incompatibility are alleviated, one must take into account expectations regarding the software, and how much one has to invest in making that choice.

Distributed Computing
The last few years have brought important changes in the area of software development, such as the creation of standards that

allowed systems to be integrated more quickly, supporting an increasing number of users and applications over the internet. With the creation of the concept of Web Services and its materialization through HTTP + SOAP protocols, the services were definitely exposed on the Internet.

Since then, concepts such as cloud computing and software as a service (SaaS - Software as a Service) have emerged. Software as a service, whether through a local infrastructure or through data centers around the world, allows application features to be offered as a service over the Internet and consumed on-demand, flexibly and dynamically.

The evolution of IT from monolithic software production systems, similar to the production systems created by Enri Ford, is clearly perceived, where the customer does not participate in the process, being only a consumer of the good produced, for software as a service, the latter being a process of intense consumer user participation.

With this increasing increase in the use of the Internet and the reduction in the prices of computers, it has contributed to the creation of a model with distributed applications, more and more, the PC and a variety of other interfaces (portable devices, laptops, phones) are used as a user interface that provides access to data and remote computing, this trend is not surprising, as a network-centric model offers significant advantages.

It promotes user mobility through access to information and services, this trend has several consequences for software engineering and architecture, for such systems a new set of challenges software architecture arise, these challenges can be efficiently addressed with the resources that cloud computing offers, the challenge is to establish a minimal architecture, capable of supporting access traffic and having resources available when needed.

Ubiquitous Computing (Internet of Things)

The third trend is related to pervasive computing in which the computing universe is populated by a wide variety of computing devices: toasters, home heating systems, entertainment systems, smart cars, etc.

In addition, these devices are likely to be quite heterogeneous, which requires special considerations in terms of their physical resources and computing power.

There are several consequential challenges for software architecture. For example, it may be desirable to have an architecture that allows you to modify the computational fidelity based on the energy reserves at your disposal.

While this may be suitable for environments where we have only a few computing devices, relatively static (such as PCs and notebooks), it does not scale to environments with hundreds of devices. We must, therefore, find architectures that provide much more automated control over the management of computer services, and that allows users to move easily from one environment to another.

The software architecture has grown considerably over the past ten years and promises to continue that growth for the foreseeable future. Many of the solutions to these challenges are likely to arise as a natural consequence of architectural practices, and other challenges arise with the evolution of computing and the needs for software: these will require significant new innovations, proposing an approach that helps manage complexity in development software. Create approaches that make it possible to visualize the system in modules and observe the relationships between them, thus making the implementation much more effective and efficient.

The architecture consists of a high-level model that allows an easier understanding and analysis of the software to be developed, to represent these solutions, the software architecture as the most appropriate solution to meet the requirements of the software, and evaluation of this structure must be fulfilled.

Organizations can obtain considerable benefits in terms of cost reduction and time to market, increasing the quality of the final product using appropriate software architecture techniques, but there are risks and costs associated with the adoption of these practices that must be evaluated before embarking in this initiative.

References

https://www.computer.org/csdl/magazine/so/2003/05/s5011/13rRU
    x0xPkQ

http://itwebtutorials.mga.edu/php/chp6/print.aspx

http://itwebtutorials.mga.edu/php/chp6/using-functions.aspx

http://itwebtutorials.mga.edu/php/chp6/include-files.aspx

https://infinitescript.com/2014/10/the-23-gang-of-three-design-
    patterns/

https://sudonull.com/post/9850

http://uml.org.cn/zjjs/pdf/1112/The%20Architecture.pdf

https://apps.dtic.mil/dtic/tr/fulltext/u2/a375851.pdf

http://citeseerx.ist.psu.edu/viewdoc/download?doi=10.1.1.387.5328
    &rep=rep1&type=pdf

www.ingramcontent.com/pod-product-compliance
Lightning Source LLC
LaVergne TN
LVHW022317060326
832902LV00020B/3522